LONDON'S TRAMS

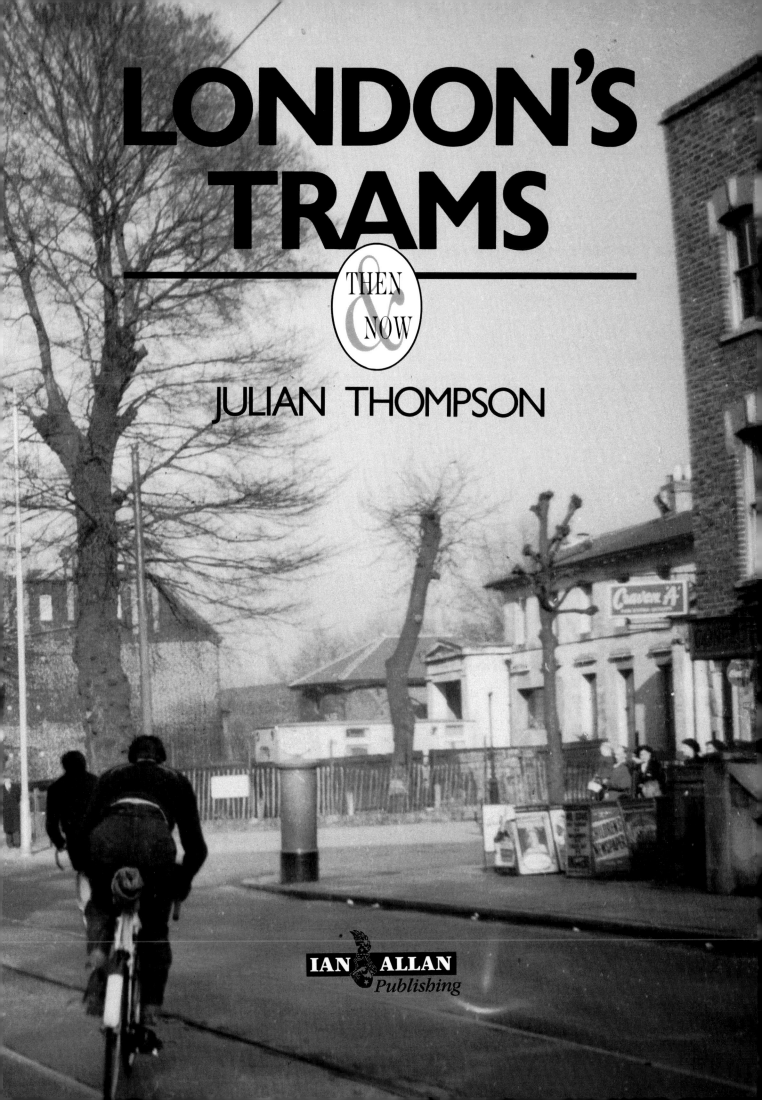

LONDON'S TRAMS

Then & Now

JULIAN THOMPSON

IAN ALLAN
Publishing

First published 1992

ISBN 0 7110 2085 X

1942 1992
IAN ALLAN
50th ANNIVERSARY

© Julian Thompson 1992

Published by Ian Allan Ltd, Shepperton, Surrey;
and printed by Ian Allan Printing Ltd at their
works at Coombelands in Runnymede, England.

A catalogue record for this book
is available from the British Library.

Previous page:
**16 March 1952: 'E/3' car
No 1956 skirts Brockwell
Park in Norwood Road at
Rosendale Road, viewed
north towards Herne Hill.**

Below:
**1 March 1952: Queen's Road
at Queen's Road station,
viewed towards New Cross
Gate with 'E/3' car No 1968.**

Contents

Foreword

This book is about the London tramways after World War 2. In treating of neglected topics, the nostalgic but often distorted view of the trams has been cast aside.

Apart from sources acknowledged, I relied greatly on notes I made while the trams were still running. All photographs were taken by myself.

My grateful thanks are due to Dr Gerald Druce for his encouragement and for information supplied. To the late Mr John Walton, who fostered my serious interest in public transport, this book is dedicated.

Julian Thompson, July 1991

PART ONE

1

The Permanent Way

Relaying the Track

The tramway route mileage from 1940 to 1950 was 101.78, of which 1.39 miles were single track. Some 75 miles were conduit operated. There were 11.16 miles of sidings and depot tracks.

Between January and mid-September 1948, 7½ miles of track were relaid, comprising 1,760 lengths of 45-ft rail weighing 2,600 tons. During 1948 the 685 permanent way men renewed 11½ miles of track.

The setts were raised with a crowbar and built up alongside the track, without interrupting trams or other traffic. The conduit yokes, the foundation of most tracks, rarely received attention. After the track had been opened, worn-out rails were replaced between passage of the trams. Rails were lifted into position with large tongs and joined with fish-plates. The D-d-d-D sound caused by the car wheels over the joints made it seem that a tram was travelling faster than it was.

At night, the opened area was protected by paraffin lamps, with a watchman in attendance. On the night of 6 February 1951, a watchman was trapped under a route 16 car in Brixton Road, apparently as he tried to rekindle a red lamp.

On conduit lines, the track and the 18in margins were sett-paved, to give easy access to the conduit. Tarred wood blocks were sometimes used, especially at pointwork. The whole track area up to the 18in margin was maintained by London Transport.

The conduit lines on the Embankment, on Deptford Creek Bridge, and at County Hall, and all overhead wire lines, were paved with tarmac. The track of overhead lines was laid on a concrete foundation, making for steadier running.

Conduit Track Construction

Over most of the route mileage, trams drew power from a channel under the track. For conduit track, a trench 7ft wide and 3ft deep was excavated. Alternate short and extended cast-iron yokes were placed at intervals of 3ft 9in, and trued up. Short yokes served to align the slot rails, and extended yokes acted also as ties for the track rails. The gaps between yokes and slot rails were blanked off, so forming a conduit when concrete was poured to the foot of the running rails.

Insulators for the positive and negative T-rails were suspended from the slot rail every 15ft, access thereto being via removable hatches. T-rails, of reversible polarity, were in 15ft lengths.

A sett surface was laid on to a layer of sand over the concrete foundation, and the joints were bound with tar. If finished with 2in of tarmac, the track was concreted up to the bottom of the railhead.

Below left and below:
12 February 1950: Due to road subsidence, the crossover in Stanstead Road at Brockley Rise had to be relaid, the work taking four weeks. Permanent way work was carried out by gangs of about six men. Power for equipment was drawn either from T-rails or from the overhead.

9 May 1987: A bus on route 171, which replaces the 35 tram route, nears Forest Hill. View towards Catford.

Right and below:

18 February 1951:
Kennington Road at Walnut Tree Walk, view towards Westminster, with 'E/3' car No **164**. Track under repair was defined by stakes wedged into the setts and linked by ropes or chains, just clear of the track area. On the approach are vertical red 'TRACK UP' banners.

31 January 1987: RM1209 on route 3. In the intervening **40** years the trees have grown considerably, although the majority of the buildings are unchanged. On the left is a bus lane, a measure designed to reduce congestion for buses — congestion that withdrawing the trams was designed to end.

24 July 1950: Short and extended yokes were 2ft 4in and 6ft 2in wide respectively, 2ft deep, and had a 16in by 16in semi-circular opening. Special large yokes were used at pointwork, which was erected on a concrete foundation. The view shows Lambeth Palace Road at New Curved Street, looking north towards Westminster Bridge Road. Behind track in the first stage of assembly is already assembled pointwork.

17 December 1988: An RTC tour bus passes the County Hall hexagon.

Operations on Conduit Track

The T-rails were interrupted at points and crossings to give the plough free passage: the dead section could be up to 12ft long. At intervals, usually at the end of an electrical section, the conduit was dead for 3ft, and ploughs could be removed through a hatch.

Removable hatches forming the conduit slot facilitated inspection of conduit point tongues, which moved with the track points. Motormen were instructed to cut off current at dead sections, otherwise the car surged when it picked up current again. On a dead section, the car lights went out, and if it stalled, it could be pushed clear by a follow-ing tram, sometimes using a timber baulk inserted between the buffers.

Usually conduit track had one slot, but in Stockwell Road and at Greenwich Town Hall, there were two slots on the single track. The conduit was often off-centre. In both cases short yoke construction was nec-essary.

All points were double-tongued, and of short radius, causing the car to lurch at speed. On sharp curves, tracks were wider spaced to allow for car overhang: the super-elevation at Westminster and Blackfriars Bridges on the Embankment was not possible on street track.

Right and below:

25 March 1950: Once the yokes were aligned into the final position, the slot rail was bolted to them, bolts in the conduit slot acting as gauges. This view east from near York Road, County Hall, shows the Addington Street track under construction.

31 January 1987: The signal box and buildings in the left background were demolished during 1990 and 1991 in works connected with the rebuilding of Waterloo station to accommodate the Channel Tunnel. The work is due for completion during 1993.

Left and below left:

3 September 1950: Trailing points in Lambeth Palace Road, looking north at Westminster Bridge Road. Track points were slightly ahead of conduit points, ensuring that the plough took its correct course: but sometimes plough and wheels took differing paths at junctions. The second yoke in the photograph is of a special angular type.

17 December 1988: A bus on route 53 passes under the bridge connecting the County Hall with the hexagon.

Top and above:
28 June 1952: The change-pit in Eltham Road at Leyland Road, viewed towards Eltham, one week before closure of the tramways. Change-pits were manned for 19hr daily: that at Woolwich was in use from 4.50am until just after midnight. There were eight change-pits on normal routes in 1950; the busiest was at Downham and the least-used that at Gresham Road, Brixton.

10 October 1988: L44 on route 122, replacing tram route 72. The houses set amongst the trees on the right have been replaced by blocks of flats.

To reduce dead sections, conduit junctions were kept simple. Dead sections were reduced by short radius curves and lack of compound pointwork. The problem of dead sections led to the adoption of traversers at depots: storage tracks were laid at right angles to the street, and connected by a moving platform, alignable with any track.

Ploughs and Plough Carriers

The plough ran transversely in a carrier under the centre of the car; it passed through a 1in-slot midway between the rails, the bottom part brushing the T-rails 14in below the road surface. Power was conducted via the carrier busbars to the motors. The plough neck was ½in wide, and snapped easily at an obstruction. Most ploughs shunted out at change-pits, where the slot was centred between the tracks. The trolleyless 'HR/2'

cars, running on conduit lines only, had long-lead ploughs plugged into the car terminals.

Change-Pits

Changeover points between conduit and overhead often had a down-grade towards the conduit; thus the car could edge forward on the hand brake when taking up the plough. Cars approaching on conduit track halted just before the change-pit, and the trolley pole was raised by the conductor standing on the track.

At Longley Road, Tooting, just after 9am on 6 January 1948, a conductor so engaged was standing between two Wimbledon-bound cars, when a third crashed into the second, and he was killed. At the inquest on the 12th, a tram driver explained: 'It is a common thing to get partial failures of magnetic brakes'. The driver of the third car stated that his magnetic brake failed to act: 'I have had absolute brake failures before,' he said. 'It is usually the case that they . . . work immediately afterwards'.

The plough slid out from under a car proceeding on to the overhead, and came to rest in a conduit slot siding between the inner rails, where the end of the conduit formed a Y. The plough was reused for cars entering the conduit section.

When a car approached on the overhead, it stopped short of where the conduit crossed to the track centre. Upon release of the hand brake, the car moved slowly forward to centre the plough, which was eased into the carrier with a pronged fork. The trolley pole was lowered, and the car proceeded after no more than one minute's delay.

Maintenance of the Conduit

The alignment of T-rails was checked with a long-handled mirror. The first sign of a defect was when a car failed to draw current: T-rails could drop out of true or buckle.

Much conduit track was unstable due to broken or subsided yokes, but the expense of reconstruction was not justified in the postwar period. Rolling and pitching of the cars could be reduced by tightening of joints, but little welding was done.

To allow for conduit cleaning, no all-night cars ran on Saturday night/Sunday morning. The conduit cleaner was a converted bus chassis with suction gear. The slot rails, 2in higher than the running rails, prevented most water entering the conduit, which drained into the main sewerage system.

Breakdowns on the Conduit System

The intense heat on 6 June 1950 twice interrupted services at Lavender Hill, Battersea, causing a four hour delay. In the afternoon a plough caught fire: castings holding the T-rails had expanded, forcing them downwards out of reach of ploughs. Later, between the Town Hall and Clapham Junction, a gang worked for three hours to rectify 180ft of faulty track. On 8 July a power failure, presumably caused by a faulty plough, halted trams for 90min between Rushey Green and Lewisham Clock Tower.

'E/3' car No 192 on route 33 had just crossed Westminster Bridge, on 3 November 1950, when its plough jammed, causing it to derail on the Embankment curve. It crossed the loading island, hit a taxi, and ended broadside across the road. A London Transport official stated: 'The people in the tram had a miraculous escape. It seems hardly possible that a tram could hit a 6in-kerb, run across an island, and still remain upright.'

Overhead Layout

The span wires were attached to poles at right angles to the track. Additional wires parallel to the tracks provided anchorage for extra span wires, enabling poles to be placed further apart. This was a rudimentary form of horizontal catenary. The overhead was led to one side under bridges, so that the trolley pole was not depressed too far, minimising risk of dewirement.

Standards were canted away from the road; bracket arms had a more pronounced rake; centre poles were found in High Street, Croydon. For each direction of travel there was a separate conductor wire. Feeder pillars at half-mile intervals bore telephones on top of the section box: the feeder cables ran up the standard and on to the span wire, where a short dead section on the trolley wire caused the merest flickering of the car lights.

The hissing sound of the trolley wheel ceased briefly at each ear, or when the wires changed direction, and caused drumming on the car roof on curves. Current was collected by a swivelling trolley wheel; an extra rope secured the wheel to the pole, and the trailing rope led off this safety rope.

All trolley-fitted cars, except older 'E/1s', had two trolley booms; one was normally secured at each end of the car, to the right-hand hook when the car was viewed from the end. Trolley ropes were fastened to a spiral attachment above the destination box, and to a cleat on the near side of the dash.

The problem of dewirement at speed was never solved. When a route 74 car derailed in Downham Way on 10 June 1948, it caused nearly an hour's delay; a breakdown tender added to the chaos when it fouled downed wires.

Tramway electricity consumption in 1948 was 94.7 million low tension units, averaging 2.78 units a car mile. This was about 10% of London Transport's power consumption for traction purposes.

The State of the Tracks

In January 1948, Deptford Borough Council considered that the defective paving of local tram tracks was dangerous. A reader of the *Croydon Times* complained in September about the 'appalling' state of the borough's tracks, despite renewal of 182 rails since the previous February. Hammering at loose joints caused paving to deteriorate, and rails were often below the level of the road surface.

Below and bottom:
18 November 1950: Merton Road at Pelham Road, with 'E/1' car No 1812 on a Saturday morning short working to Stockwell station. On the left-hand standard is a semaphore light signal, apparently not working. Two horizontal lights indicated 'LINE OCCUPIED', and two diagonally 'LINE CLEAR'. Signals were actuated and cleared by overhead line contacts.

30 April 1988: DMS 2353 on route 80. Amidst all the changing street scenery it is interesting to note that the People's Dispensary for Sick Animals still occupies the corner it did 40 years ago.

2

The Rolling Stock

The Rolling Stock Situation

Of about 1,000 trams in stock in 1945, some 150 were stored at Cressy Road, Hampstead. By the end of 1948, 862 cars were in stock; their total seating capacity was 61,956, most cars seating 73 or 74 passengers.

The 333 modern cars comprised the 'Feltham', 'HR/2', and 'E/3' types, and car No 1. Wooden-bodied cars made up the rest: 93 were of Croydon, East Ham, West Ham, and Walthamstow origin, and some 440 were 'E/1s' of various types. Some eight basic types became 20 if one included subclassifications.

The 'UCC' or 'Feltham' Type

After the war, there were still 98 standard 'Felthams', dating from 1930-31, and also prototype car No 2167, which had a lower canopy and dash.

'Felthams' had 64 seats, and room for 10 standing in each vestibule. The driver's separate cab was cramped. Straight staircases gave quick and safe loading. Magnetic brakes were fitted, but the air brake was used for service stops: its inexpert application caused flat wheels.

Seats on both decks were divided and luxurious. The longitudinal seats at the end of the top deck, one of which curved round the end of the car, gave a poor view forward. The top deck saloon appeared lengthy due to absence of bulkheads, and the windows had glass louvres.

The car interior was designed for passenger flow. After collecting fares on the top deck, the conductor regained the lower by the front staircase. The front exit doors were used only by the driver after the war, whereas the rear doors remained opened for boarding and alighting.

Two 70hp motors were fitted; all axles of the maximum traction trucks had roller bearings. A 'Feltham' could reach 40mph, but its performance on hills was poor. Very steady riding, the typical motion was a side-to-side rolling.

The 'HR/2' Type

Introduced in 1930-31 for hilly routes, 51 cars of the '100' series, and 39 of the '1800' series were in service after the war.

The all-metal body was of 'E/1' layout. The lower deck exterior was flush-panelled, and the 74 seats upholstered in rexine, but some cars had cloth upper deck upholstery. Some 'HR/2s', including No 120, had swivelling bucket seats downstairs.

The handbrake was fitted with a wheel, to enable it to be screwed down before descending Dog Kennel Hill. The 'HR/2' tended to side-to-side rolling. Each axle of the equal-wheel trucks was driven by a 35hp motor, giving a maximum of 40mph.

The 'E/3' Type

The 'E/3' entered service concurrently with the 'HR/2', and had an identical body. The

Below and below right:
18 November 1950: 'Feltham' car No 2143 leaves the Victoria Embankment by the curve on to Westminster Bridge in the Saturday midday peak. View looking west. Telford Avenue was the only depot with suitable clearances for 'Felthams'. They ran on routes 8, 10, 16, 18 and 20, and from June 1949 also on routes 22 and 24.

28 January 1990: T852 on route 12. Traffic lights have replaced the policeman on point duty, but the traffic island on the left retains the lamp standards from 40 years before.

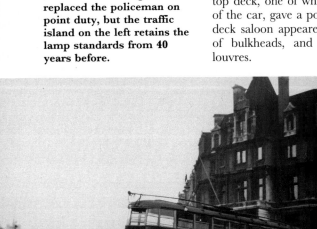

'1900' series had no windscreens as delivered, but the '100' series had 'HR/2' pattern metal cabs. Two 57½hp motors were fitted to the maximum traction trucks, with roller bearings on all axles. The 'E/3' had a steady motion, and could reach 35mph. There were 143 'E/3s' in postwar service.

The 500 series 'E/1' Type

There were 48 of these cars after the war. They had new bodies mounted on the trucks of former types 'F' and 'G'. The two 42hp motors fitted made them slow compared with other cars. The '500' series 'E/1s' were much used on routes 68 and 70, and could also be seen on all other New Cross depot routes except 35.

The 'E/1' Type

The standard 'E/1' was built between 1907 and 1913, with a final, very similar batch in 1920-22. This most numerous type of car numbered some 400 units, of which 134 were rebuilt cars. The four-window saloon body was of wooden construction. The maximum traction trucks were fitted with two 42hp motors, in the case of the '1800' series with two 60hp motors.

Platforms were small, and the driver's windscreen could be opened for ventilation. A nearside driving mirror, adjustable by a lever to the driver's left, was fitted. A chain closed off the platform at the driving end, and also the rear platform, if the car was full: an 11-year-old girl was killed when she failed to board a full tram in Streatham High Road in November 1948.

The 18in-wide, 90°-turn staircase was not easy to climb. The door at the top was kept open, but that at the driving end remained closed. A single sliding door, opening towards the stairs, shut off the platform from the lower deck. The offside saloon bulkhead and end door had yellow-tinted glass, to reduce glare for the driver at night.

Downstairs were 27 seats, and on top 46. Lower deck seats had cloth upholstery. The two longitudinal seats at each end of the lower deck gave ample room for standing passengers, but no more than eight were carried after the war — for a time it was reduced to five. The longitudinal seats contained sand hoppers; the sand was dropped on to the rails if the driving wheels slipped.

Top deck seats were generally upholstered, but some cars still had wood-slat top deck seats until about 1950. Of the two longitudinal seats at each end of the top deck, that on the offside at each end was cramped, as it followed the curve of the car end. One could sit at the very end of the car, a good viewpoint, and higher than a bus, but here the pitching was felt most.

All transverse seats could be turned to face the direction of travel. The conductor turned the seats at the terminus. The main top deck windows were of half-drop type, moved in unison by rack and pinion. Sliding windows at both sides at the top of the stairs enabled the conductor to check passengers at stops. The lower saloon had opening lights above the fixed windows.

As there was no bell on the top deck the conductor gave the signal to start by stamping on the floor over the driver, or by blowing a whistle.

Internal painting was dark brown to window sill level, and white above, including ceilings, which were slatted. Some '1800' series cars, including No 1841, had a smart dark blue paint scheme instead of brown.

The 'E/1', very free on its springs, gave a smooth ride over good track, but pitched severely over bad. Pitching and swaying were reduced by a full load; some drivers also tightened the handbrake to this end.

Top and above:
8 September 1951: Blackfriars Road at The Cut, view towards Blackfriars, with 'HR/2' car No 132. The '100' series 'HR/2s' were the only cars in the fleet without trolley poles and most had metal-framed windscreens.

11 October 1987: M977 on route 63. The railway bridge remains largely unchanged — except for the loss of the advertisement — but is now surrounded by modern office blocks.

16

Far left, top and bottom:
17 July 1951: Southwark
Bridge terminus from the
south in the evening peak,
with 'HR/2' car No 1860. The
'1800' series 'HR/2s' had
wood-framed windscreens,
and a different pattern of
truck to the '100' series.

31 May 1987: Today no buses
cross Southwark Bridge on
Saturdays or Sundays. The
large multi-storey car park is
perhaps indicative of
changed priorities.

Left and below:
18 August 1951: Peckham
Rye terminus in Peckham
Rye at Elland Road, with
rebuilt 'HR/2' car No 127.
'HR/2' Nos 1884, 1885, 1887,
and 1893 were also rebuilt.
Note the partially blanked-
out three-line destination
indicator.

3 July 1987: Today, the
prefabricated and Victorian
houses have gone, to be
replaced by modern houses
and flats.

The 'E/1' and all other London trams were fitted with hand and magnetic brakes with wheel attachments. A Pre-1914 'E/1' could reach 30mph, and an '1800' series car about 35mph. The latter could always be recognised by the roof level route number. Croydon, East Ham, West Ham, and Walthamstow cars were very similar to the 'E/1'.

The Rebuilt 'E/1' Type

Starting in 1935, 145 'E/1' cars were modernised; most were still running after the war. The cars were rebuilt with flush-panelled sides, recessed route and number indicators, and windscreens. The top deck seats were upholstered, and the interior brightened up, but the basic layout was unchanged.

Streamlined 'E/1s' and 'ME/3'

Some 'E/1s' were rebuilt to a more pleasing design: cars Nos 2, 982, 1103, 1260, and 1370 had inward-leaning top deck pillars and rounded roofs of pleasing appearance. Still more handsome was 'ME/3' car No 1444. Only car No 2 ran until the end of tramway operation.

'K' Type — Ex-Walthamstow Corporation

Cars Nos 2042-2053 were built in 1927, and 2054-2061 in 1931-32. The 1927 cars had platforms projecting further than usual beyond the top deck, and low platform aprons. The 'K' type was noted for very springy seats, of which there were 69. Two 63hp motors gave a top speed of 40mph.

'WH' Type — Ex-West Ham Corporation

These cars were built in 1925-31. Two 50hp motors gave a top speed of some 25mph, though Nos 334-343 were remotored in 1946-47. Of 32 West Ham cars in stock after the war, two were used as staff cars. Seating capacity of the differing batches was between 69 and 73.

'EH' Type — Ex-East Ham Corporation

The 20 East Ham cars built in 1926-27 all saw service in postwar London. They were similar to the '1800' series 'E/1s', but with roller blind route number indicators. Two 60hp motors gave a good performance.

The saloon roof panels were decorated and varnished; car No 83 had stained glass windows in the lower deck. The seating capacity was 71.

'CCT' Type — Ex-Croydon Corporation

After the war there were 23 Croydon cars running. Nos 379, 380, and 398 were rebuilt in the same way as 'E/1s'. All cars had two 65hp motors, giving a good performance, and were reputedly well built. The cars dated from 1926, and seated 69.

Below and below right:
8 April 1851: Greenwich Church Street terminus, view north from near Nelson Road. The end top deck windows of car No 840, one of the oldest 'E/1s' still in service, have been strengthened with H-irons.

14 March 1987: The quiet backwater has become a busy one-way street, although many of the earlier buildings remain.

Car No 1

The prototype of an intended fleet of 100 cars, No 1 appeared in 1932. It was 36ft long, 2ft longer than a standard London County Council tram. Air brakes were fitted, and the seated driver had a separate cab. Four 35hp motors drove equal-wheel axles on trucks similar to those fitted to the '100' series 'HR/2s'.

Very comfortable two-and-two transverse seats were fitted on both decks; the total capacity was only 66. Straight staircases gave access to an upper deck without bulkheads, but the lower deck platforms were small.

Car No 1 always worked from Telford Avenue depot after the war. For a time, it ran only on all-night services. From about 1949, it could be seen working in the peak between the Embankment and Thornton Heath Pond, and sometimes on routes 22 and 24.

External Bracing of 'E/1' and Similar Types

Many wooden-bodied cars, mostly '1800' series 'E/1s', were fitted with external bracing in 1949-50. Lower deck bracing consisted of metal rods fitted diagonally from the platform end of the window sill to the centre of the main frame, on both sides of the car. H-plates also reinforced the upper deck window frames.

Trucks and Running Gear

All cars except the 'Felthams', No 1, the 'HR/2s', and the 'E/3s' ran on Maguire-pattern maximum traction trucks. The kingpin, connecting the car body to the truck, was offset towards the driving wheels, which bore two-thirds of the car weight. The pony wheels, or inner small wheels, served to guide the truck, and were prone to derailment.

The maximum traction trucks of the 'Felthams' and 'E/3s' had roller bearings to reduce rolling resistance. The weight on each 'HR/2' axle was equal, as the kingpin was centred over the truck.

The magnetic brake shoe with lead was placed between the axles on both sides of each truck. Older pattern maximum traction trucks were secured to the car body by chains at each side. Axle boxes could be opened for greasing.

Tram buffers were sprung by dint of their semi-circular form, and could absorb light shocks. The standard buffer height made it dangerous to pass between closely drawn up trams. Only 'Felthams' had a buffer placed before the dash: they were flimsier, and often hung crooked.

Trams could thus push each other, but car overhang on curves made this more difficult; here, a series of short nudges was the rule. Even trams full of passengers often pushed one another long distances: when a route 72 car arrived at Beresford Square, Woolwich

Right and below right:
**1 April 1951: New Cross
Road at Pepys Road, view
towards Greenwich with 'E/1'
car No 1817, followed by
rebuilt 'E/1' No 1619.
No 1817 has diagonal lower
deck bracing.**

**26 September 1987: RM973
and 2099 on route 36B
replacing the 54 tram (left);
and T931 on route 171 in
place of the 35 tram (right).**

Far right, top and bottom:
**18 November 1950: Ex-
Walthamstow car No 2052 at
Purley terminus. This car
carries Cheap Midday Fares
boards, and is fitted with
diagonal lower deck bracing.
Note the deep canvas strip
below the windscreen.**

**29 September 1988: LS168 on
route 166.**

with a smoking controller on 10 February 1952, it was pushed to Abbey Wood depot by a 46.

The lifeguard at each end of the car was connected to a lifeguard tray set 4in above rail level, before each truck. If the lifeguard was tripped, the tray fell to the ground, causing a pedal on the platform to rise; it could be reset by depressing the pedal. Nearside lifeguards under each platform were often omitted latterly. A lifeguard filled the gap left by the off-centre plough carrier of the 'Feltham'. Lifeguards were of wooden slats.

The Magnetic Track Brake

All cars except the 'Felthams' and car No 1 used the magnetic brake for service stops. With the controller handle on the brake notches, the motors acted as dynamos, energising track brake shoes suspended just above the rails. The backward drag of the magnets actuated brake blocks on the driving wheels.

At the same time, the rheostatic brake altered the flow of current to the motors, also helping braking. During rapid deceleration,

the controller emitted a coughing sound, and use of the magnetic brake was accompanied by a high-pitched whine. At night, the magnets gave off showers of sparks. Experienced drivers eased off the magnetic brake at low speed and brought the car to a smooth halt with the hand brake.

Magnetic brake failures resulting in accidents often occurred after the war. On gradients the hand brake was largely ineffective, so reliance was placed on the magnetic brake; its failure in such locations led to some of the worst accidents. The magnetic brake kept the rails smooth, but wore them out quickly.

Air Brakes

Car No 1 and the 'Felthams' were fitted with compressed-air brakes for service stops, but also had magnetic and hand brakes. Inexpert use of the 'Feltham' air brake caused flats on wheels; the cars were often driven using the magnetic brake.

'Feltham' air brakes were latterly fitted with quick air-release, which emitted a loud, brief hissing sound as the car was about to

Far right, top and bottom:
22 June 1952: Abbey Wood terminus from the south, with ex-West Ham car No 344, and 'E/3' No 176 in the background.

21 September 1986: Much-widened Knee Hill today.

move off. The experienced drivers of car No 1 knew how to apply the air brake.

Driver's Platform and Controls

The controls consisted of a controller which governed the flow of current to the motors, and actuated the magnetic braking system. The controller was an upright metal box with resistances and contacts, and a handle on top. To accelerate, the driver moved the handle to the top series notch, giving a speed of 15mph; further clockwise movement through the parallel notches raised the speed to 30-40mph.

At rest, the handle was in the ten o'clock position; in top series at one o'clock; and in top parallel at five o'clock. In braking, the handle returned anti-clockwise through the power notches, for the first brake notch at nine o'clock, and the last at six o'clock.

One of three positions could be obtained with the controller key: on; off; or reverse. Trams were rarely reversed, as they could be driven from duplicate controls at each end: the driver had easy access to the interior of the car, in contrast to many buses today. The controller handle could remain untended on any notch while the driver performed other activities.

The hand brake was a tall braced staff to the driver's right, its handle being level with that of the controller. It was applied by winding clockwise. At the same time the driver brought the pawl at the foot of the staff into contact with a ratchet. Hand brakes acted only on the driving wheels. 'HR/2' cars had a wheel in addition to the handle, so that greater leverage could be obtained when screwing down the track brake blocks before a steep descent.

The driver freed the handbrake pawl by a clockwise motion of the handle, or by kicking it free of the ratchet. Between controller and hand brake was the gong pedal, and in front of it, the lifeguard tray pedal.

An 'A' or 'B' painted inside the dash signified differing electrical arrangements at each end of the car. Here could also be found the last overhaul date: for instance, '5/49' showed that the car had been overhauled in May 1949.

The driver's step was always raised, but on 'HR/2', 'E/3', and later 'E/1' cars it folded. 'Felthams' and car No 1 had fixed steps. The circuit breaker and plough-to-trolley changeover switch were under the stairs. The circuit breaker tripped with a loud bang when acceleration was too rapid, and had to be reset at once to avoid a run-back. Other platform equipment under the stairs included a point lever, car tool box, and spare plough.

Tramcar Colour Scheme

Tramcars were painted in a slightly darker shade of red than today's buses. All window frames and the blank panel in the windscreen were cream; the large cream areas possibly made the red appear darker.

Cream and red were divided by black lining; there was also black lining above the lower deck ventilators, and along the top and bottom of the windscreen. 'E/3' and 'HR/2' cars were enhanced by deep lining below the cab roof, and vertical lining on the windscreen window frames.

The dashes were lined with fine yellow stripes. Above the headlamp appeared the stock number in gold edged in black, the only application of Gill Sans script to the trams. Stock number and car type appeared at the bottom of the rocker panel next to the platform, in black until late 1949, then in white. For the whole postwar period, the fleet name 'LONDON TRANSPORT' was carried in gold with black edging, centrally on the waist panel.

'Felthams' had no platform lining. There was a broad black band below the lower deck windows, and a large cream area above. No changes were made to the tramcar colour scheme after the war.

Destination Equipment

All unrebuilt standard cars had external destination blind boxes. To save material, some wording was common to more than one destination: 'CLAPHAM' was common to 'DEPOT CLAPHAM' and to 'CLAPHAM COMMON STATION'. 'E/3' blinds, illuminated from the front, because the same light source was used for the 'VIA KINGSWAY SUBWAY' slide, were harder to read at night than rear-illuminated blinds. The recessed indicators of rebuilt cars allowed for three-line blinds, but on most cars the top of the indicator glass was blanked out.

Standard cars carried side route boards, white with black lettering, giving termini and about six intermediate points. Reversed, the boards showed 'CHEAP MIDDAY FARES', with white lettering on a red field. Dog Kennel Hill route cars carried an extra board 'TO AND FROM KING'S COLLEGE HOSPITAL', with white lettering on a blue field. Kingsway Subway cars had a 'VIA KINGSWAY SUBWAY' board, also white on blue.

Route Number Display

Unrebuilt 'E/1' cars had route number stencils pierced to allow light to shine through. The large white-backed route number stencils fitted to 'E/3', 'HR/2', ex-Croydon, ex-Walthamstow, and '500' series 'E/1' cars, were changed by opening the front top window inwards.

The distinctive Croydon Corporation stencils lasted until the end of the Croydon routes. Towards the end of the tramways, new stencils were needed as cars were transferred to routes for which none existed: 12, 22, 24, 34, 36, 38, 46, 54, and 74.

Above and right:

8 July 1951: Southwark Bridge terminus, looking north, with ex-East Ham car No **86.** Behind the tram are temporary ramps bridging bomb damage. The roof of Cannon Street station is seen on the right.

19 September 1988: The new City skyline. The bomb-damaged roof of Cannon Street station was eventually dismantled, with offices built over the tracks in its pace. The tower of Wren's St Michael Paternoster Royal is one of the few constants in this **40-year** period.

Ex-East and West Ham cars had separate route number boxes, and those on rebuilt 'E/1s', 'HR/2s', and ex-Croydon cars were recessed. 'Feltham' route number boxes were flush with the top deck nearside body-work.

Conventional cars in full route regalia showed route numbers at both ends, on both sides, and on the side route boards.

Charlton Works

On the north side of Woolwich Road, just east of Tunnel Avenue, was situated Charlton Works. There was a track connection from the Angerstein Wharf branch, which formed the western boundary.

A tram received an overhaul every two or three years. A steady stream of cars could always be observed as having had attention, but repainting did not always mean stripping off all old paint.

In 1948, 92 light repairs, and 332 heavy repairs and overhauls, were carried out. At the end of the year, 52 trams awaited repair in workshops, and 72 in depots and yards.

The 147 cars noted as having been over-hauled in 1949 were: 66 'E/1s'; 24 'HR/2s'; 17 'Felthams'; 16 'E/3s'; 10 ex-West Ham; 8 ex-Croydon; 2 ex-East Ham; 1 ex-Waltham-stow; and Nos 2, 1444, and 1597. In 1950, 108 newly overhauled cars were noted.

The State of the Trams

By 1950, most 'E/1s' showed signs of ageing; pitching contributed to loosening of the body, especially around lower deck bulkheads, and at the upper deck ends.

London Transport was reported on 17 November 1950 as stating that defective trams should be taken out of service. It denied a *South London Press* report that men at New Cross depot were refusing to drive leaky trams, but confirmed that the previous week 48 trams returned to the depot with leaky cabs.

Value and Modernity of Rolling Stock

The gross book value of the 862 trams at the end of 1948 was £2.09 million. Even then, the 'Felthams' could still be regarded as modern; they had a better layout than today's buses, and gave a smoother ride.

Cleaning of Trams

Tramcars were cleaned manually inside and out. Exterior cleaning suffered latterly, but Holloway and Thornton Heath depots had a good standard. The duckboard flooring was hard to clean, and upholstery was often threadbare.

In July 1951, London Transport stated: '. . . our system of cleaning has not been relaxed . . . The upholstery is regularly vac-uum cleaned, . . . at this late stage in the life of the trams it would be wasteful to spend any more money on new upholstery'.

Noise and the Trams

The main source of tram noise was bad gear-ing, notably on the ex-Walthamstow cars. Flat wheels were common to all types of car, es-pecially those from New Cross and Norwood depots.

Much noise at points and crossing was inevitable with the conduit system. While raised-grooved crossings were possible for running rails, there could be no raised-groove over the conduit slot. The conduit channel also acted as an echo chamber. Trams pass-ing over mechanical joints in bad repair caused a great deal of clatter.

In January 1949 the Balham Chamber of Commerce agitated for replacement of all-night trams by buses, due to the noise caused. A trader whose shop had been robbed said that thieves had waited for a passing tram to drown the sound of breaking glass. London Transport refused to run buses, as there was no garage on the route, but agreed to instruct crews to reduce running noise.

Top and above:

25 March 1951: South End at Parker Road. 'E/3' car No 1906 on route 18 waits for ex-Croydon car No 397 on route 42 to reverse. On the left is an RT on route 59. View north towards central Croydon.

10 April 1988: A route 68 bus nears its terminus at South Croydon garage. The sign for the car parks and the new office block tell their own story.

3

Operation of the Tramways

The Tram Routes

The 800 trams in daily service amounted to 8½% of London Transport's road fleet. Some 60 cars were always being repaired or overhauled.

Twenty-seven routes ran daily, but four were curtailed on Sundays. Ten routes were weekday only, five of these running only in the peak. Unusually route 62 was cut back from Savoy Street to the Elephant and Castle on Saturday afternoon and evening, but extended from Forest Hill to Lewisham Clock Tower: this working survives as bus route 185A. Southwark Street alone had no Sunday service.

The longest routes were 35, 16/18 and 36/38: 13¼, 13 and 12½ miles respectively, with running times of 86, 78 and 75min. Thirteen routes had a journey time of one hour or more. The shortest routes were 42 at 20min and 44 at 21min.

Closest headways were on routes 36/38 east of the Elephant and Castle and on routes 42 and 54. Routes 16/18, 40, 56/84 and 58 had a 4min interval; most other routes ran at least every 6min.

Peak Hour Extras and All-Night Cars

Extra peak hour cars strengthened services on routes 16/18, 36/38 and 72. Route 16/18 cars carried 'EX' instead of a route number, and the others bore an 'X' suffix.

The six all-night routes did not run Saturday night/Sunday morning. A homeless woman told the Clerkenwell Magistrate on 29 December 1945, that she had been sleeping on all-night trams. Asked: 'Have you been doing that every night?' she replied: 'Yes, for about three weeks.'

The two all-night routes based on New Cross depot combined to give a 15min interval between there and Savoy Street: route 5 running via Old Kent Road and route 7 via Walworth Road. In June 1946, all-night routes received their final numbering: 1, Tooting Circular via Embankment; 3, Battersea-Blackfriars; 5, Downham Way-Savoy Street; 7, New Cross-Embankment; 26, Clapham Junction-Westminster; and 35, Highgate-Bloomsbury.

The first weekday car to leave a depot in the morning was the 3.33am route 46 car from New Cross to Eltham Church, only three hours after the last car of the previous day, on route 40 from Woolwich, had returned.

The Busiest Junctions and Tramways

Vauxhall was the busiest junction with 270 cars passing in the peak. Other junctions with more than 200 cars an hour, in descending order, were: Elephant and Castle; Camberwell Green; Oval; Waterloo Bridge; County Hall; and New Cross Gate. The tramway with the most cars passing in both directions in one hour in the peak, was Waterloo Bridge to County Hall, with 226 cars an hour.

Many main sections of tramways had at least 70 cars an hour: this frequency extended as far as Tooting Broadway, Goose Green, Grove Park and Woolwich. The longest intensively served section was Victoria-Grove Park.

Improved Services

From 29 October 1947, routes 12, 68 and 74 were improved in the peak, and routes 12, 56/84, 66, 70, 74 and 78 at other times. Route 31, previously Battersea, Princes Head-Westminster (Bloomsbury in the peak), ran from Wandsworth to Islington Green on weekdays, but ended at Westminster on Sundays. Route 72 became Woolwich-Savoy Street all day on weekdays: previously it ran to Savoy Street only in the peak, ending at New Cross Gate in the slack, as it still did on Sundays.

Passenger Journeys and Car Miles Run

Trams carried 301,518,000 passengers and ran 34,024,000 car miles in 1948, increases of 6.6% and 3.7% over 1947. Of passengers carried and vehicle miles run by London Transport, the tramway share was 5%. Each tram in stock ran 40,000 miles a year on average.

Alterations to Tooting Routes

From 19 October 1949, routes 2/4 were cut from 30 to 24 cars an hour between Wimbledon and Kennington; during November, peak hours extras with duty number 25 to 28 were seen going to Blackfriars only. From the 19th also, route 6 terminated at Tooting Broadway instead of Tooting, Amen Corner. From this time until routes 2 and 4 ceased, Saturday afternoon extras were run from Wimbledon to Stockwell, a feature continued at first by replacing buses.

The Festival of Britain Footbridge

The Embankment at Charing Cross closed to

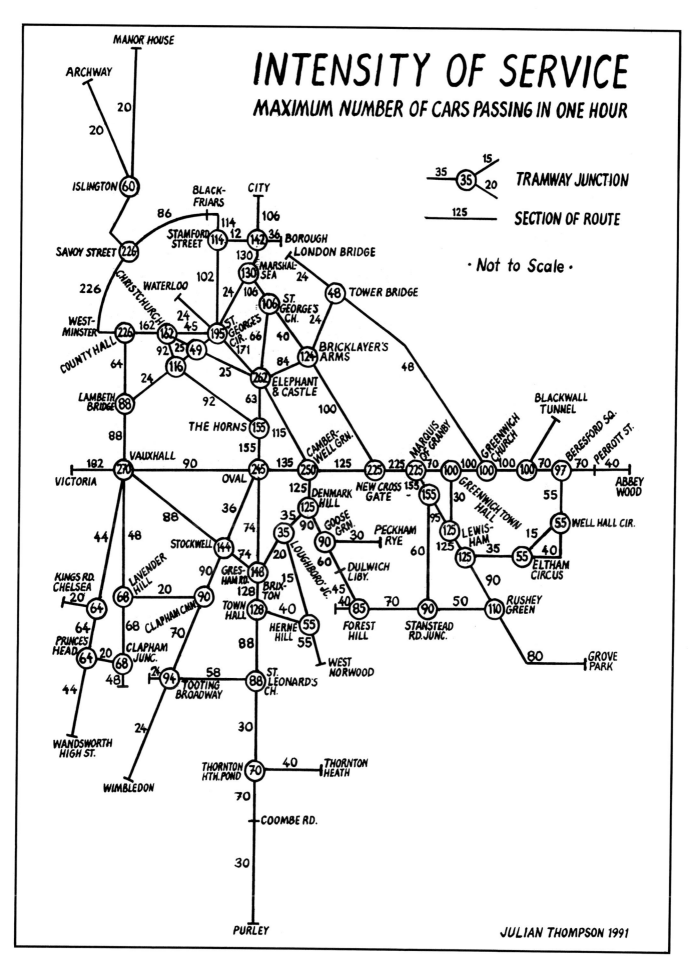

INTENSITY OF SERVICE
MAXIMUM NUMBER OF CARS PASSING IN ONE HOUR

TRAMWAY JUNCTION

SECTION OF ROUTE

· Not to Scale ·

JULIAN THOMPSON 1991

Top and above:
16 July 1950: 'E/3' car No 183 on route 33 reverses in Borough Road at St George's Circus, to continue via Lambeth Road into Kennington Road. It was diverted during closure of the Embankment at Charing Cross.

28 January 1990: A Boro' Line bus on route 188 at St George's Circus. This route has now returned to London Transport operation.

trams and other traffic from 7pm on Friday 14 July 1950, for completion of the Festival of Britain bailey bridge across the Thames. Trams via Westminster terminated at New Scotland Yard, and those via Blackfriars at Savoy Street. On the 16th, a few continued to Charing Cross, returning on the wrong track; ex-Walthamstow cars Nos 2058 and 2060 ran a shuttle service to that point.

Trams entered and left the Kingsway Subway on the wrong track. All three Subway routes ran via Blackfriars to St George's Circus, the 35 continuing down London Road. The 31 and 33 reversed in Borough Road, continuing along Lambeth Road, the 33 using the curve into Kennington Road.

On 17 July the first tram passed under Charing Cross Bridge at 8am: the Embank-

ment was again closed for 12 hours from 6pm, for completion of the bridge.

The Trams in Adverse Weather

After the war, there were still 20 snow-brooms, single deck cars with raised bodies and a broom at each end, but no wind-screens. They carried a dummy plough to free the slot from ice and snow.

During the winter of 1946-47, the only severe winter of postwar tramway operation, slush froze over the conduit slot, breaking ploughs. On 28 January 1947 trams in the Forest Hill area were delayed by frozen points.

On the night of 28/29 January contraction of the slot broke many ploughs. Serious delays occurred at New Cross Gate and in the Old Kent Road, completely disrupting services.

On the 31st, a diverted route 18 car came to rest across icy tracks at Clapham; at midnight on this day, all trams left depots with an extra sack of sand for use on gradients.

In the early postwar period, about 15 million tons of coal were burned annually in London by domestic and industrial users. This resulted in 'pea-soupers' that often developed from mid-afternoon: visibility might decline to 20yd and not exceed 50yd for days on end. Only the trams kept going in the densest fogs, which made bus and trolleybus operation difficult or impossible. During a week-long fog in 1948, when drivers could see only a few yards of track in front of their trams, they did well to reach the Embankment from Balham station in 45min.

Stopping Places

Trams stops were usually placed at the approach to traffic lights, making it easy for passengers to cross the road. Stops for opposite directions were close to each other.

Many London County Council stop signs lasted until 1952. The commonest was of trefoil shape; there were also a few oblong brown and yellow signs. The last London United Tramways stop sign, with white lettering on green, was removed from the northbound stop in The Broadway, Wimbledon, at Stanley Road, in the summer of 1950.

Many stop signs were of prewar standard pattern, bearing the word 'TRAMWAYS' in a bar-and-circle; both compulsory and request stops were cream. The first new standard stop signs were erected in the spring of 1949. Compulsory stops had a white field, and request stops blue.

Large illuminated signs at many points on routes 2 and 4, as at Clapham Common, had all gone by April 1949. During the last week of trams on any route, portable stops signs replaced the old tram stops. Stops for replacing buses were hooded until the first day of the buses.

Left and below:

30 March 1952: The eastern entrance to Holloway depot, from Pemberton Gardens. The overnight snowfall of 29/30 March 1952 was one of the few heavy falls of the postwar tramway period.

2 July 1988: Renamed Highgate upon conversion to buses, this garage is now Holloway again! Demolition of the building in the right foreground has allowed the access to the depot to be widened.

Right and below:
22 June 1952: Plumstead High Street at Riverdale Road viewed towards Abbey Wood, with ex-East Ham car No 87. The stop signs are of London Transport prewar standard pattern: above, tram; below, trolleybus.

13 December 1987: L70 on route 269. A petrol station has replaced the terraced housing on the right, whilst the police station remains largely unchanged — even the sign over the door is present 35 years earlier.

Far right, top and bottom:
1 July 1952: Lewisham Way at Breakspears Road, with 'E/3' car No 1939, four days before the system closed. View towards Lewisham. The bus stop sign in the foreground is hooded until the trams cease.

31 January 1988: T1070 on route 36.

It could be hazardous to step into the road to board a tram; other traffic was not obliged to stop. When a tram neared a stop, the conductor extended his arm as an indication to other traffic. Even when a tram was stationary, vehicles might try to nose their way through a throng of passengers.

A girl about to board a tram was knocked down by a lorry in Mitcham Lane and seriously injured on 11 October 1947. On 6 December 1949 a girl was injured by a motor cycle, as she returned to the pavement, on learning that the tram was a short working, in Camberwell Church Street.

At Charing Cross on 19 June 1950, a woman trying to board a tram not at an official stop was dragged a few yards. She was awarded £151 19s damages with costs against London Transport!

Tramway Telephones

In 1947 there were 4,500 London Transport telephones. The system was equivalent to the GPO network in a town the size of Brighton. The tramway and trolleybus telephone system was very extensive. Tramway telephones were found on the top of section boxes.

Trams and Traffic

Petrol was rationed until 1950, when traffic conditions immediately deteriorated.

The predictable path of the trams in the road centre was appreciated by cyclists. The tracks and sett-paving were sometimes blamed as a source of skidding.

It was usually possible to overtake a tram on the inside, due to the absence of parked vehicles. Trams kept traffic on the proper side of the road: to pass one on the offside was dangerous.

In June 1951, South London councils were studying a report that traffic conditions had worsened since 1947, and that scrapping of all trams would bring further deterioration. Average traffic speeds had fallen from 11.1mph in 1947 to 10.5mph in 1951. Private cars accounted for 32% of traffic; commercial vehicles for 39%; and trams and buses for 29%. The busiest main road in Lambeth, Kennington Park Road, bore 1,192 vehicles an hour in both directions.

But 1951 flows were small compared with today's. Critical points were at Westminster and Blackfriars Bridges, where traffic crossed side-running tracks as they regained the road centre.

Tram, trolleybus, and bus schedules varied little for similar routes. The average London tramway speed of 10.4mph was higher than on most British systems. But crawling drivers were common.

Speed Restrictions

Occasionally '4MPH' was painted in white between the rails, as at the Blackfriars facing crossover. Drivers were instructed to shut off current at dead sections, and slow down at facing points. Excessive speed at facing junctions was the cause of serious accidents. In June 1947 two bad collisions occurred at County Hall, resulting from false setting of points: the precise circumstances remain obscure.

Seven people were injured on 17 June 1947, when a route 36 tram was switched into the path of an Embankment-bound 33 at County Hall; the fronts of both were smashed, the 36 suffering severe damage. On 22 June a route 62 car was diverted head-on into a route 16 at the same point; both were damaged, but no one was hurt.

Sharp curves were subject to speed restrictions. Cars rounding curves on the overhead system had to slow down, to avoid dewirement of the trolley pole.

The Tramway Accident Record

From 1946 to 1951 inclusive, 225 trams, of which 93 were damaged, were involved in 181 accidents. Ten persons were killed, and 373 were injured. There were no passenger fatalities.

The worst months were October 1948 and August 1950, with 10 accidents and seven collisions each. The worst year was 1950, with 40 accidents, the second highest number of injured (74), and the most fatalities (three).

Of 65 persons injured in 1947, 40 were in two collisions in May: on the 20th at St John's Hill, Clapham Junction; and on the 29th at London Road, West Croydon. Of 119 injured in 1951, 71 were in three collisions: on 2 July at Lewisham Way (the worst postwar accident with 32 injured); on 26 August at Christchurch, Lambeth; and on 11 September on the Embankment.

In 1948 London Transport paid almost twice as much compensation to tramway passengers as to trolleybus passengers, but there were twice as many trolleybuses as trams. About 16% of all compensation was for tram accidents.

Multiple collisions were common. On 17 March 1947 five trams collided on the Embankment: the ends of all were damaged. On 26 November 1949 13 people were injured when five trams collided in London Road, Elephant and Castle. Flying glass caused many injuries: in February 1949, Camberwell Council urged the adoption of safety glass.

Tramway Publicity

There were five postwar issues of the tram and trolleybus map, the first in 1946, and the last in 1950. The maps gave first and last vehicles, running times, frequencies, and time-tables of all-night routes.

Tram stops gave no service information, and few bore route numbers. Times of first and last cars were displayed in tram shelters.

4

Finances, Labour Relations and Fare Structure

Tramway Finances

The trams lost £1,058,774 in 1948, 18% more than in 1947. Fares were lower than those charged on London buses, and working expenses higher than on most British tramway systems.

Receipts for 1948 were £2.65 million, and expenditure £3.71 million. Expenditure of 26.19d a car mile was 7.5d more than takings: operating costs were 16.88d; maintenance and depreciation 7.22d; and general expenses 2.09d.

High maintenance costs reflected the difficulty in keeping obsolete equipment working. The working loss did not include provision for repayment of interest on capital, with which London Transport was still burdened.

One-Day Strike at Telford Avenue

On 10 August 1946, 443 drivers and conductors at Telford Avenue depot struck for one day. No trams ran from Brixton to Norbury or Tooting. The strike was against the advice of the Transport and General Workers' Union. London Transport stated that it arose from the men's complaint about the state of the tramcars: everything was being done to restore the cars to prewar efficiency.

An Inter-Union Dispute

It was reported on 26 August 1946 that 12 tramwaymen at New Cross depot had not worked since 27 May, but still drew pay. They were members of the National Passenger Workers' Union: crews belonging to the Transport and General Workers' Union would not work with them.

London Transport warned that unless they joined the T&GWU by 1 September, the Board would have to dismiss them. Although the NPWU obtained an injunction against London Transport on 6 September, the men were eventually forced to join the T&GWU.

Tram Crews' Wages After the War

Crews worked an 11-day fortnight. At the beginning of 1947, a conductor started at £5 16s a week, rising in instalments over two years to £6 5s. The 44-hr week consisted of six turns of 7hr 20min: 6hr 25min were spent on the car, the rest being reporting and paying-in time.

The wage differential whereby tram crews had earned 4s a week less than bus men was abolished by giving tram men 2s a week more from January 1951, and a further 2s from January 1952. By October 1951, the basic starting wage for a tram driver was £6 16s 6d; for a conductor, £6 12s 6d.

The Saturday Afternoon Pay Dispute

Tram crews struck on 1 January 1949 for extra pay for Saturday afternoon work. Only trams from Thornton Heath depot were running. By the end of January, time-and-a-quarter had been granted for Saturday afternoon work on trams and buses, at an extra cost of £375,000 a year. Tramwaymen received 8½d an hour more.

Daily Performance and Running Numbers

The average daily miles scheduled for tram and trolleybus crews in 1948 were 64.3 from Monday to Friday; 65.2 on Saturday; and 67.5 on Sunday.

Duties were numbered from 1 upwards on each route, pairs of routes such as 2/4 counting as one route. The duty number was a dark blue enamelled plate with white figures, carried in a bracket inside the windscreen to the left of the driver, and in the same position at the other end of the car.

Adjustment to the timing of late-running cars was made by short-working. After the war it was regular practice for drivers to crawl in order to be turned at a recognised point.

The Conductor's Work

Conductors carried a leather bag for cash; the float on starting duty was about 3s. His fibre box contained ticket rack, spare clips of tickets, waybill and clipboard, and sandwiches. Before joining the car, he would have read notices regarding his duty.

The Bell Punch ticket canceller, in use until the end of the trams, clipped on to a belt which fastened over both shoulders. The punch cut a circular hole in the ticket, denoting the point to which one was entitled to travel. The punched material could be analysed should there be a discrepancy in paying in. The numerous concessions and transfers demanded a good knowledge of the fare structure.

Tramway Jargon

The conductor moved down the car calling 'ENNYMOREFAHSPLEES', and might be heard to refer to 'ROUT 2'. If the lower deck was full, one was asked to travel 'OUT-SIDE'. It was the conductor's job to swing the 'POLE', and reverse the 'BOARDS'.

New Cross was known as 'THE GATE', the Kingsway Subway as the 'TUNNEL', and trams using it 'TUNNEL CARS'. According to the conductor, the tram might be going to the 'EPHELANT' or 'WESTMINISTER'.

The driver 'NOTCHED UP' or 'DOWN'; a sudden 'NOTCHING DOWN' attracted the 'ANCHORS' to the rails. A pitching tram might trip the 'GATE' or 'UNSHIP' the 'TRAY'. Rapid acceleration tripped the 'BREAKER' with a loud report.

A late-running tram was so many minutes 'DOWN': the driver might 'DRAG THE ROAD' in order to be 'TURNED SHORT'. Delays might be caused by a tram stuck on a 'DEAD', or a 'SHORT' in the plough, which had to be removed from its 'CARRIER'. A car with a 'HOT BOX' had to be 'RUN OFF' at the 'SHED'. Often trams were sent to 'CRD' for overhaul.

Excavated track was referred to as 'UP', but officially it was 'OPEN'. Men working on the 'UP' and 'DOWN ROADS' were 'GANGERS', who included 'PAVIORS'.

The Tramway Fare Structure

The following refers to the tariff in force from 9 February 1947 to 30 September 1950. Thereafter, all transfers and returns were abolished.

Ordinary Single Fares Without Transfers

Ordinary 1½d and 2½d Singles had no transfer entitlement except in the Croydon area.

Ordinary Single Tickets with Transfers

All tickets except the 1½d and 2½d Single carried transfer facilities, allowing one change of car to reach a destination, even if a through service existed. A 5d Transfer issued at Balham station on a route 6 car going to Southwark Bridge allowed one to change at Stockwell for Victoria, the Embankment or Southwark Bridge; or at the Elephant and Castle for the Embankment.

How Transfer and Return Tickets Were Punched

Transfer tickets were issued for journeys between Central London and suburban termini and for cross-suburban journeys. For a Transfer, tickets were punched above the double line on the front or back. Single tickets were punched in the destination space, and Returns at 'A' or 'B', according to where change was permitted. The reverse bore a list of transfer points.

Transfer and Return tickets were cancelled below the double line with a punch that left a small hole and perforated numbers and letters. Transfers were cancelled on the second car, and Return and Workman tickets on the return trip. A ticket was punched four times for a return journey with transfers in both directions.

Specimen Fares from Blackfriars, 1945-50

	Westminster	Stockwell	Clapham Common	Balham	Tooting Broadway	Wimbledon
May 1945	1½d	2d	3d	4d	5d	6d

9d Return (Tooting Broadway–Wimbledon)
3d Cheap Midday (Balham–Wimbledon)

	Westminster	Stockwell	Clapham Common	Balham	Tooting Broadway	Wimbledon
Feb 1947	1½d	2½d	4d	5d	6d	7d

3d Cheap Midday (Clapham Common–Balham)
11d Return (Tooting Broadway–Wimbledon)
4d Cheap Midday (Balham–Wimbledon)

	Westminster	Stockwell	Clapham Common	Balham	Tooting Broadway	Wimbledon
Oct 1950	1½d	3d	4d	5d	6½d	8d

6d Cheap Midday (Tooting Broadway–Wimbledon)

Examples of Rate Charged per Mile in 1945

Ticket	Journey	Pence	Pence/mile
Ordinary Single	Blackfriars-Wimbledon	6	0.62
Ordinary Return	Blackfriars-Wimbledon	9	0.46
Cheap Midday	Blackfriars-Wimbledon	3	0.31

In 1945, bus and Underground fares averaged 1.0d per mile.

Examples of Cross-Suburb Transfers

Journey	Change at	Fare
Blackwall Tunnel-Grove Park station	Lewisham Clock Tower Catford	11d Return
Forest Hill-Grove Park station	Catford	5d Workman Return
Wimbledon-Harrow Road Scrubs Lane	Tooting Broadway (to trolleybus)	4d Cheap Midday

The Maximum Fare

The modified London County Council fare structure lasted until 30 September 1950. Maximum fare was latterly 7d, with 11d Return. These tickets were valid between London termini and suburban termini in the LCC area, and also to Wimbledon. London termini were Bloomsbury, Victoria, Southwark Bridge and the Embankment.

The longest journey using the 7d Single and 11d Return was Blackfriars-Abbey Wood (13.25 miles) at a rate of 0.53d a mile Single and 0.42d Return. The tickets were issued all day, except when replaced at certain times by Cheap Midday and Workman Return fares. Routes 31, 33 and 35 had a special tariff.

Cheap Midday Fares

The Cheap Midday fare from 1947 to 1950 was 3d for 4d and 5d Single; and 4d for 6d and 7d Single. The tickets were issued on trams leaving Central London between 9.30am and 4pm and those arriving between 10.30am and 5pm.

Workman Return Fares

Workman tickets were issued until 8am, for return at any time of day. The Return fare between Wimbledon and the Embankment was 8d for a round trip of 19.5 miles.

Exchange Tickets

Between 12 and 25 June 1949 Transfer tickets were surrendered on the final journey against no-value Exchange Tickets. This test of the use of Transfers led to their withdrawal from 1 October 1950.

Luggage Facility

For a 2d fee, passengers were entitled to convey items on the front platform of trams, under the driver's supervision. No such facility has ever existed on buses.

Colourful Tram Tickets

According to the amount of printing they bore, tickets varied in length from 2in to 5in. Values up to 2½d bore stage numbers only, but all route 34 tickets were stage printed. Tickets were of hard white paper, overlaid with coloured strips down each side, leaving the centre third white. The super-imposed colours were richer than those of bus tickets, which were of coloured paper.

The colours of tram tickets from 1947 to 1950 were: 1d child, lobster; 1½d, white; 2d child, apple green; 2½d, blue; 4d, blue/green; 5d, brick red; 6d, light brown; 7d, violet; 11d Return, khaki brown; 3d Cheap Midday, pink; 4d Cheap Midday, blue/green; 8d Workman Return, yellow/orange; and 9d Workman Return, pale brown. Other Workman tickets were the same colour as the same value single ticket, eg the 5d Workman Return was brick red.

From 1945 until 1947, the 5d Single was light brown and the 6d pale yellow. Ticket shades varied: the 5d Single from cherry red to bauxite, and the 11d Return from light khaki to dark slate. Fare value overprint was usually red, and the diagonal stripe of Workman issues green.

2d Minimum Fare Rejected

A public enquiry, which opened on 2 July 1946, rejected a 2d minimum fare from 1½ miles of travel. The new fare scale was approved on 4 November, and came into force from 9 February 1947.

The Trams and Workmen's Fares

The nearing end of the trams raised fears of fare increases. On 14 December 1949 it was reported that tram replacement might mean the end of workmen's fares, issued only on trams and trolleybuses. Over 800,000 tram passengers a week used cheap fares. In four weeks ending October 1949, workmen's fares on trams and trolleybuses yielded £107,000, and ordinary fares £759,000.

On 3 March 1950 it was stated that objections to proposed new fares had to be lodged with the Transport Tribunal by the 28th. Workmen's fares would be replaced by Early Morning fares, which would also be issued on buses. The 2½d fare for journeys over two miles would increase to 3d. Revenue would increase by £3,500,000 a year.

Various London borough councils had voiced opposition, followed on 21 March by the London County Council, and on the 22nd by the Trades' Union Congress.

The 1950 Fares Tribunal

When the Tribunal opened on 9 May, Mr Lionel Heald KC, for the British Transport Commission, said that under the fares scheme, 600,000 people using Workmen's tickets would pay more, but 250,000 bus travellers would pay less. A new Early Morning Single fare, dearer than existing workmen's tickets, would also be issued on buses. Mr Heald referred to Workmen's tickets as an 'anomaly': one class of passengers was subsidised by another.

On 19 May Mr R. Reader Harris MP, for the London Passengers' Association, claimed that the 3d Workman Return would rise to 5d, and the 4d to 6d. He suggested on 6 June that some of the increase in working costs was due to tramway abandonment. When he asked if it were not possible to postpone the scheme, Mr Valentine claimed that the trams were on their last legs.

On 14 June Mr W. A. H. Parker, consulting engineer of Craven House, Kingsway, suggested that the trams should be retained, and not replaced by buses, 'as they are the more economical of the two to operate'.

The Fare Increases of 1 October 1950

From 1 October 1950 the 2½d and 6d fares increased by ½d, and those of 7d and above by 1d. As the highest value ticket was 8d, two tickets were issued for fares over 8d. All tickets bore stage numbers only: the exception appears to have been the 6d brown Cheap Midday, which showed some 18 tram and trolleybus termini. Routes 33 and 35 had a separate ticket issue.

Transfer and Return fares were abolished; the new 6d Cheap Midday was issued for 6½d and 8d Singles, but gave cheaper travel only on far longer rides than hitherto. The Workman Return was replaced by a 2d Early Morning Single, with return at normal fare: these tickets were issued on all London Transport road services.

A Comparison of Fares Then and Now

The single fare from Wimbledon to the Elephant and Castle has increased as follows:

	1950	1991	Increases
To South Wimbledon station	1½d	40p	64 times
To Longley Road, Tooting	2½d	50p	48 times
To Balham station	4d	50p	30 times
To Clapham Common station	5d	50p	24 times
To Stockwell station	6d	70p	28 times
To Elephant and Castle	7d	(70p)	24 times

In 1950 tram routes 2 and 4 ran through to the Embankment, for which the fare was also 7d. Today, the 155 bus runs from Wimbledon to Vauxhall via Stockwell. The fare to the Elephant and Castle is conjectural.

4d Cheap Midday, 1947.

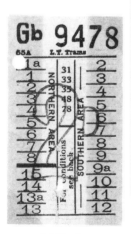

3d Cheap Midday, 1945-47.

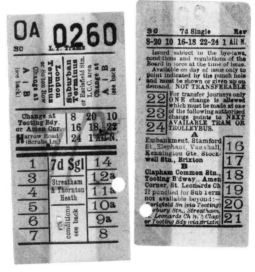

7d Maximum Fare, 1947.

4d Single, 1947-1950.

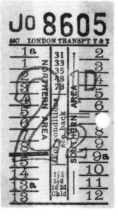

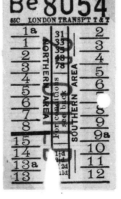

2½d Single, 1947-50.

2d Single, 1945-47.

1d Child Single, 1945-1947.

2d Child Single, 1947-50.

PART TWO

5

The North London Routes

The Kingsway Subway

Connecting the Embankment at Waterloo Bridge with Bloomsbury, the Kingsway Subway was two-thirds of a mile long. Under Aldwych the tunnel was partly single and partly double; the last sharp curve was divided by a central wall. Between Aldwych and Holborn was double track. Much noise was caused by running over corrugated track and over crossovers, which were located at the southern portal, both sides of Aldwych station and south of Holborn station. The dim lighting added to the eeriness. From Westminster to Bloomsbury, 7min were allowed, and from Charing Cross five.

On Sundays the Subway attracted joyriders. At island platforms at Aldwych and Holborn stations, passengers used the front platforms of trams. The stations had indirect roof lighting, and walls and central pillars tiled in white and light green. Station signs, similar to those on the Underground, were visible from both decks. Over each 6in-high platform hung signs giving points served.

Beyond Holborn station, a short down-gradient was followed by twin-tunnels. A 1:10 ramp led up to the junction of Theobalds Road and Southampton Row. On the sharp curve into Theobalds Road were contacts in the conduit slot: combined with contacts at Holborn station, these actuated light signals for cars entering and leaving the Subway — the ploughs of northbound cars set the signal at Holborn station, and cleared it at Theobalds Road; those of southbound cars set the signal at Theobalds Road and cleared it at Holborn station.

Above right and right:

5 April 1952: The southern portal of the Kingsway Subway, under the Embankment arch of Waterloo Bridge. Police-operated lights enabled trams to enter and leave the Subway. 'E/3' car No 184 on route 35 to Forest Hill is about to leave on the last day of operation.

3 January 1987: The sealed entrance to the Kingsway Subway. After closure the subway was used for a number of jobs, including acting as headquarters for London's Civil Defence, and is now owned by Camden Council.

Bloomsbury

Trolleybus routes 555, 581 and 665 had a sharp curve into Red Lion Square terminus. In the 150yd to New North Street there were three facing crossovers; in barely two miles from Waterloo Bridge to Islington Green 12 crossovers were provided, possibly a record for London. Sometimes trams marooned on a dead section used trolleybus overhead; this was unauthorised, for the rails of conduit track were not bonded.

Rosebery Avenue and its Viaduct

Rosbery Avenue between Grays Inn Road and Farringdon Road is on made ground. Warner Street is crossed on a viaduct, with steps down to the street below. The underside of the viaduct is of barrel-vault brickwork, the spacing of the inner four girders roughly corresponding to that of the rails of a double track tramway.

The Islington Green Lay-By

On the west side of Islington Green, north of the Essex Road/Upper Street junction was a lay-by for route 31 cars. It formed a trailing junction with the northbound track, crossed over the southbound, and rejoined it at the Essex Road junction.

Holloway Road and Highgate Archway Terminus

Trams reached good speeds on the wide and straight Holloway Road: many an exciting race took place with a trolleybus on the parallel stretch of route 609 between the Angel and Highgate. On 31 January 1947 a broken plough caused 29min delay in Holloway Road.

Just beyond Upper Holloway station, a 200yd-long double track connection led along Pemberton Gardens to Holloway Depot; it formed trailing junctions with the tracks in Holloway Road, where on 7 February 1951 a derailed tram caused a big delay.

The double track terminus with facing crossover was just north of Archway station, in Highgate Hill at MacDonald Road.

Green Lanes and Manor House

In Green Lanes was a section of single track at Springdale Road. Beyond Clissold Park, a steady climb towards the terminus passed filter beds on the west, and two large reservoirs with ornamental pumping station on the east.

At North London Magistrates' Court on 4 January 1949 a tram driver admitted dangerous driving in Green Lanes on 18 October 1948. He had hit a reversing lorry, which then killed an elderly lady, and was fined 40 shillings with three guineas costs.

The double track at Manor House ended just short of a disused change pit. Usually only the west track was used for standing, but on occasion trams were parked side by side. North of the Manor House Inn, on the east side of Green Lanes, is still a section of sett-paved track at a former permanent way depot.

Depot Allocation of Cars on Routes 33 and 35

'E/3' cars were used on Kingsway Subway routes; sometimes 'HR/2s' could be seen on route 35. Unusually, 'E/1' car No 1393 from Norwood depot was noted on route 33 in the morning peak of 22 June 1950, even though wooden-bodied cars were banned from the Subway.

Route 33 cars were based on Holloway and Norwood depots, and those for route 35 on Holloway and Camberwell. All but seven of the 23 'E/3s' at Holloway on 30 September 1950 were of the '100' series. Holloway depot also accommodated 230 trolleybuses. Wandsworth and Holloway were the only joint trolleybus and tram depots.

Fast Runs on Routes 33 and 35

A fast run logged on 16 December 1951, from West Norwood to Manor House on 'E/3' car No 169 from Holloway depot, took exactly one hour for 11 miles. On the last day of route 33, 5 April 1952, 'E/3' car No 180, also from Holloway, took 58min and averaged 11.38mph for the same run.

The fastest recorded run on route 35 was on 11 March 1951 from the Elephant and Castle to Highgate in 35½min, an average of 10.98mph.

Present-Day Replacements of Routes 33 and 35

Route 33 north of Bloomsbury is covered by bus 171A, and route 35 north of the Angel by routes 43 and 263A. Bus route 171 runs from Aldwych to Islington Green, Monday-Friday only. All-night route 35 from Bloomsbury to Highgate is covered by bus route N92.

The Link from Holloway Depot to Hampstead Store

Trolleybuses on the Hampstead and Parliament Hill Fields routes used the rear exit of Holloway depot, via Monnery Road, into Junction Road. This exit was one end of a 2¼-mile tramway to Hampstead Store, situated in Cressy Road, near Hampstead terminus.

Reduced to single track, it ran via Fortess Road, Kentish Town Road, Prince of Wales Road, Malden Road, Southampton Road, and Fleet Road. Many trams stored at Hampstead were destroyed by fire in 1947. The connection was last used about 1949.

Parts of the line, including the Cressy Road entrance tracks, were still to be seen in the mid-1950s. The old depot, essentially unaltered, is used today by the London Borough of Camden. A former London County Council Tramways office block still fronts Cressy Road.

Right and below:
5 April 1952: 'E/3' car No 1993 bound for Manor House climbs the Bloomsbury ramp only 10hr before the Kingsway Subway closed. The Subway between Lancaster Place and Kingsway at Sardinia Street was adapted and opened for small vehicles in 1964.

5 July 1987: Tracks remain today on the Bloomsbury ramp.

Left and below:
3 February 1952: Dorset Street (now Dove Road) from Essex Road, with 'E/3' car No 1946. View looking east. Northbound trams used Dorset Street, and those southbound Balls Pond Road. At the junction of Dorset Street, southbound cars passed over the northbound track; at Mildmay Park, northbound cars crossed the southbound track.

13 November 1988: M1165 on replacing route 171A.

6

The Victoria Embankment

Below and below right:

30 December 1951: The Victoria Embankment at Blackfriars viewed west from John Carpenter Street. Ex-Walthamstow car No 2052 is about to leave for Grove Park. In constructing the Blackfriars Underpass, the line of the Embankment at the bridge was straightened. Plane trees and old lighting standards were removed as far as Temple Avenue.

3 January 1987: RM450 on sightseeing duty. Closest to the camera, the former tramway alignment now provides other road transport with a link down from Blackfriars Bridge.

The Busiest London Tramway

Between County Hall and Waterloo Bridge, 226 cars an hour passed along the Victoria Embankment, the most intensively served London tramway. Beyond Savoy Street, where many routes terminated or diverged, the flow dropped to 86 an hour.

Taboo for other traffic, the tracks had a tarmac surface. Occasional islands separated them from the westbound roadway: islands at Westminster, Charing Cross, Savoy Street and Temple served for boarding and alighting; that at Westminster was extended southwards in June 1949. Collisions occurred between trams and other traffic on the Embankment on 6 April 1946 and on 19 June 1950.

Seven minutes were allowed for the 1¼ miles from Westminster to Blackfriars. Westminster and Blackfriars each had two crossovers; that nearest the bridge at Blackfriars was facing, giving a run-round facility. Cars reversed at Blackfriars on the John Carpenter Street trailing crossover. Other crossovers were just south of Charing Cross and east of Waterloo Bridge.

Permanent Way Work on the Embankment

Much work was done on the tracks during 1949: in January, the track at Charing Cross loading island was relaid, and in February the westbound east thereof. Both tracks east of Waterloo Bridge were relaid in February. In March, the outer curve at Blackfriars was relaid and in June the inner. The eastbound near the Blackfriars facing crossover was relaid in July and both tracks opposite Temple station in August/September.

In April 1950, much of the eastbound between Charing Cross and Savoy Street was relaid. The inside curve at Westminster was renewed in February 1951. In April, the Savoy Street and Charing Cross crossovers were relaid.

Buses Share the Tram Tracks

From October 1950 the inner Embankment track was also used by buses. Buses were

slightly wider than trams and had to hug the kerb and so could not overtake. Some plane trees had to be lopped or removed. Buses in the other direction used the roadway.

Accidents on the Embankment

On 11 September 1951 an eastbound route 56 tram collided with, and overturned, a bus on route 170 leaving Temple Place. At least 14 persons were injured. Both vehicles were badly damaged, the bus falling across the tracks with a smashed roof and cab. Mr H. Ford of training ship *Wellington* stated '. . . it was as if the bus had struck a mine. It stood on end, turned completely round, and then crashed on its side'.

Also at Temple Place on 27 September an eastbound route 38 tram collided with a route 170 bus. The tram derailed, collided with a van, and blocked both tracks. Two bus passengers were injured.

Terminal and Stopping Arrangements at Waterloo Bridge

All eastbound trams at Waterloo Bridge used the island at the Kingsway Subway entrance. The westbound stop for Subway cars was west of the bridge, and that for other cars east of it.

The reversal point east of Waterloo Bridge was known as 'SAVOY STREET': this street is actually west of the bridge. Savoy Street terminus was used by routes 22, 24, 40, 62 and 72 from Monday to Saturday; and on Sunday only by routes 26, 40 and 56. In the peak, 30 cars an hour reversed there.

Blackfriars

There was a gentle northward curve before the sharp curve on to Blackfriars Bridge. At the point of transition was an entrance to a pedestrian subway, where, until the trams ceased, a sign directed passengers to 'LCC TRAMS'.

The Embankment at Blackfriars suffered from subsidence; the distortion of paving, and to some extent of track, was most noticeable near John Carpenter Street, but was never remedied.

The Embankment Tramway Replacements

Nineteen tram routes used the Embankment on weekdays and 14 on Sundays. Only six of these routes have a present-day bus equivalent that reaches either Blackfriars or Westminster: the 59/109 bus, ex-16/18 tram; 45 bus, ex-34 tram; 177EX bus, ex-36/38 tram; and 184 bus, ex-56 tram.

The 184 bus, the last replacing route to run the full length of the Embankment, runs via Westminster Bridge and returns via Blackfriars Bridge in the early hours of Monday-Friday only. The 59 runs Monday-Friday, the 109 Monday-Saturday, but the 177EX Monday-Friday peak hours only. The 45 bus runs daily, and is the only replacing route to touch the Embankment on Sundays (at Blackfriars), but now runs only to Brixton.

Above and right:

10 May 1952: The Victoria Embankment from Waterloo Bridge viewed towards Blackfriars. 'E/3' car No 1913 has just left Savoy Street terminus, which is beyond the trees on the right. There was kerbside loading on the river side of the road. This arrangement presented some danger: fatalities to pedestrians occurred on the night of 25/25 July 1948; and on 30 May 1950.

28 November 1987: RMA51 on a sightseeing tour. With the abandonment of the trams the opportunity was taken to use the area occupied by the trams to widen the road. Behind, the river frontage of Somerset House forms an attractive backdrop; until the construction of the Victoria Embankment in the 19th century the River Thames ran up to the base of the façade.

Above and left:

18 November 1950: 'E/3' car No **171** stops at Westminster during the Saturday midday peak. For southbound passengers at Blackfriars, there was a shelter at John Carpenter Street and a larger shelter nearer the bridge, the latter used by all trams in the slack hour. A third shelter on the riverside pavement at Blackfriars was similar to that at Westminster, seen here.

28 January 1990: A privately-operated London tour bus passes along where trams used to run. The demolition of the tram shelter has opened up the view of Hungerford Bridge in the background.

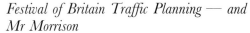

7

The County Hall

The Traffic Situation at County Hall

Until 1950, serious traffic congestion occurred at the east end of Westminster Bridge and at the York Road junction. Both tracks were on the north side of the bridge; east thereof, eastbound traffic crossed them to gain the nearside lane. The problem was partly due to the alignment of the new Westminster Bridge of 1862, with 58ft-roadway and 13ft-pavements: it was upstream of the old, and not in line with Westminster Bridge Road, which was never widened in the tramway era to match the width of the bridge.

Below and bottom:
28 January 1951: View east across Westminster Bridge, with 'Feltham' car No 2154.

6 February 1988: RML2449 on route 12. St Thomas' Hospital, on the right, has been rebuilt and extended.

Festival of Britain Traffic Planning — and Mr Morrison

Planning for the 1951 Festival of Britain started in 1948. Yet in 1949 it was uncertain if the tramways at County Hall would be remodelled; on 10 February Mr Herbert Morrison, President of the Council, apologised to the House of Commons for the need to relay the tracks there: most people, he claimed, were looking forward to the end of the trams, but the abandonment could not be accelerated. Mr Morrison, instrumental in the formation of London Transport, thus showed that he had always favoured removal of the trams.

Construction of the North Side of the Tramway Layout

A new single track was to be built from the eastbound in Westminster Bridge Road, along York Road, Addington Street and southwards to rejoin the eastbound near the cab road to Waterloo Station. The war-damaged remains of Gatti's Music Hall were cleared in 1950 for the new road south of Addington Street.

By 1 March a triangular single track junction had been laid at the east end of Addington Street and was being concreted. Track south of Addington Street had been assembled by the 30th, and work was well in hand on that in Addington Street towards York Road. By early May, the track in York Road had been concreted to form the conduit; the Addington Street siding and track south thereof had been macadamised.

Construction of the South Side of the Tramway Layout

In mid-May 1950 work started on a curved track across Stangate Green. Next, a single track was laid in Lambeth Palace Road, southwards to join existing track. By the end of August this track and pointwork on the east side of Stangate Green were nearly completed.

At the junction of old and new southbound tracks in Lambeth Palace Road existing track was excavated over a great length, due to the acute angle of bifurcation. With the current still on, at this and other such locations, the track was supported on concrete blocks, and secured with timber wedges and baulks.

The north end of Lambeth Palace Road had been widened on the east side. Towards

48

Left and below:
11 March 1950: Work started early in 1950 on a derelict site north of Westminster Bridge Road, with the construction of a triangular junction at the east end of Addington Street. This view west towards County Hall shows the exit points from the Addington Street siding.

3 January 1987: When this photograph was taken, one could still see where siding, points and curve were lifted. The site is now occupied by works in connection with Waterloo station rebuilding.

Right and below:

9 May 1950: County Hall, York Road, viewed towards Waterloo station. New track is concreted up to foot of rail level. By mid-May, both ends of the new north side track had almost reached Westminster Bridge Road.

1 February 1987: Today's bridge to the County Hall annexe does not improve the view.

Far right, top and bottom:

28 May 1950: Westminster Bridge Road at New Street, view towards Westminster, with rebuilt 'E/1' car No 1579. By the beginning of June, existing eastbound track at York Road and New Street was excavated and supported on concrete blocks, revealing short yoke construction.

11 April 1987: A route 77 bus is dwarfed by the County Hall annexe.

Left and below left:

11 June 1950: The northern part of the County Hall layout opened to outward-bound trams and other traffic on the morning of 11 June 1950. Inward-bound trams still used the old line. Ten days later, the disused eastbound in Westminster Bridge Road was removed. 'HR/2' car No 1874 turns into York Road at the Westminster Bridge Road points.

27 September 1986: RM1753 on route 53 passes the County Hall annexe.

hour only line in London, was served by routes 22 and 24.

The Addington Street Siding

There were no special trams to the Festival of Britain: the site was bounded by York Road, the river, County Hall and Waterloo Bridge. The main Festival buildings were the 366ft-diameter Dome of Discovery; the 295ft-high cigar-shaped Skylon; and the Festival Hall, since altered.

The 50ft-long Addington Street siding, rarely used and too short for terminating cars, did not justify the expense of three sets of points. Nor were cars often reversed on the layout: but on 10 August 1951 an inward route 72 returned to South London after traversing the whole layout.

The Completed Layout

Almost equally divided between north and south sides, the layout consisted of 2,250ft of single track. Of nine sets of points, only four were used by service cars. After January 1951 none of the points were needed for normal working. Running over raised-groove point-work was excellent. The track had a tarmac surface, with very few insulator inspection covers.

Transformation at County Hall

Since 1952 the County Hall one-way scheme has been remodelled. The west end of Westminster Bridge Road is now wider than the bridge. The hexagonal County Hall annexe straddles the former centre of Westminster Bridge Road.

The area south of County Hall has been rebuilt, involving demolition of fine houses. Stangate Green, formerly protected by Parliamentary Act, is occupied by the rebuilt St Thomas' Hospital.

Lambeth Palace Road runs north to south to Royal Street; the maximum deviation 400ft east of the old Lambeth Palace Road marks the southern limit of the new County Hall tram tracks. The new alignment turns south-west to join the old Lambeth Palace Road 500yd south of Westminster Bridge Road. Near this point, inside the south end of the Hospital complex, can be seen a disused part of the old Lambeth Palace Road.

the end of August new track was extended from the east side of Stangate Green, along Lambeth Palace Road, towards Westminster Bridge Road, where pointwork was being assembled at the beginning of September. Pointwork, made by Hadfield of Sheffield, was delivered with instructions as to intended location; it incorporated raised-groove crossings and conduit slot channelling.

Connecting curves were laid in the southern part of the layout, making possible reversal of cars from the Westminster direction, using the south side; and from the Lambeth North direction, using the whole layout. A south-to-east curve in Stangate was inserted after the layout opened; it was being built at the beginning of December 1950.

Use of the South Side Tracks

The south side tracks were fully used only until 7 January 1951, when the last Albert Embankment routes closed. The Albert Embankment track, sole example of a peak

Above and left:

24 July 1950: The points from Lambeth Palace Road into New Curved Street, in the background, viewed looking southwest. Construction started on the south side tracks in mid-May 1950 with the laying of a curved track on Stangate Green; this track had been concreted two months later.

27 December 1988: The site of Stangate Green, today occupied by St Thomas' Hospital.

Above and right:
22 October 1950: 'E/1' car No 1838 rounds the curve from Westminster Bridge Road into Lambeth Palace Road on the first day of the south side of the County Hall layout. It was opened late in the afternoon of 22 October 1950; at 4.45pm a test car ran over the Westminster Bridge Road-Lambeth Palace Road Curve (beyond the tram), intended for route 22 and 24 cars only.

5 November 1988: RM2187 on route 12 passes the extended County Hall.

8

Inner South London

St George's Circus

The road layout at St George's Circus was completed by 1770. In 1907 the obelisk in its centre was replaced by a clock tower, itself demolished in 1937, but the tram tracks were never rearranged. The obelisk still stands at the junction of St George's Road and Lambeth Road.

Trams often stalled on the many intersections at St George's Circus. There was a north-to-east curve from Blackfriars Road into Borough Road and a west-to-north curve from Lambeth Road into Blackfriars Road, both single track.

The Rush Hour Diversion Avoiding London Road

Southbound evening peak cars were often diverted at St George's Circus, via Borough Road, Lancaster Street, Southwark Bridge Road and Newington Causeway, to the Elephant and Castle. The northbound track in Lancaster Street and in the south end of Southwark Bridge Road were not in use. Two short sections east and south of the Borough Road/Southwark Bridge junction had no service. Lancaster Street south of Borough Road is now blocked by a Borough Polytechnic extension.

The Elephant and Castle

The war-damaged public house, now demolished, was on an island site at the end of Walworth Road. Because of war damage, the Elephant and Castle lost its former importance as a shopping and entertainment centre: the South London Palace, in London Road and Thomas Wallis' store, in Newington Causeway, were destroyed.

One of the tramway junctions was near the Bakerloo Line station in London Road, the other near the Northern Line station in Walworth Road. A north-to-south single track connected Newington Causeway with Walworth Road; from Walworth Road, northbound cars passed along Newington Butts and crossed into Newington Causeway.

At the Northern Line station, northbound routes 35, 56 and 62 joined Newington Butts and then turned into St George's Road, where the double track was used only in the westbound direction. Outward, these routes used London Road, and crossed into the end of Walworth Road, where the single south-

bound track conflicted with traffic flow — a much-criticised arrangement.

Burst Water Mains in Newington Butts

At midnight on 29/30 March 1949 a burst water main in Newington Butts flooded basements. All-night trams were diverted via Walworth Road. By 9am on the 30th, trams were running northbound only, and other traffic was diverted, but trams were normal in the evening. During repair work, the rails were supported on concrete blocks.

On 7 March 1950 another main burst in Newington Butts. Trams had to be diverted again two days later, to facilitate repairs.

Newington Causeway

During road works in Newington Causeway in 1952, probably during lifting of the tram tracks, foundations of a Roman road were found 4ft below the surface.

On 10 January 1950 three women were trapped between passing trams in Newington Causeway, and a route 6 car passed over the foot of one of them.

Southwark Bridge Road

A buckled plough caused a 50min hold up in the morning peak south of Southwark Bridge on 23 November 1946.

Ten people went to hospital on 21 December 1949, when a route 52 tram collided with a tram on route 10 in Southwark Bridge Road at Southwark Street.

Inner South London Termini

There were four termini in the area: at Waterloo, Southwark Bridge, London Bridge (Borough) and London Bridge station. The last three were within half-a-mile of each other.

Southwark Bridge Terminus

The present Southwark Bridge, second narrowest river bridge crossed by trams after the war, was opened in 1921; the 42ft-roadway is narrower than that of Southwark Bridge Road.

After the war, trams terminated on the bridge itself: the end of the line at Southwark Bridge, cut back due to the war, was never restored.

Of six services terminating, only routes 10 and 46 ran at all times. Routes 6, 52 and 60 were peak hours only, and 48 terminated at

Far left, top and bottom:

3 November 1951: London Road, Elephant and Castle, with rebuilt 'HR/2' car No **1890**, view towards St George's Circus from Princess Street. In the evening peak, long lines of trams waited in London Road for the police-operated lights to change.

16 August 1986: A bus on route 177 replacing the 36/38 tram. Apart from the road itself, there is little at this point remaining from the scene 40 years ago.

Left and below:

21 May 1950: A tram passenger's view of Newington Butts, Elephant and Castle, looking towards Blackfriars from the Northern Line station. On the right is the Elephant and Castle inn, and in the centre background the end of London Road. There was a large bombed area at the junction of St George's Road. No rebuilding was done during the tramway period.

14 March 1987: RM2001 pictured on route 12. Much of the scene has been dramatically altered – clearly visible is the loss of the Elephant and Castle Inn – but at least one building at the end of London Road remains.

24 February 1952: Walworth Road at Draper Street, looking north, with 'E/3' car No 169 closely followed by an RTL bus on route 48, introduced in January 1952 in place of tram route 48.

16 August 1986: The realigned north end of Walworth Road. The Shopping Centre occupies the old alignment.

St George's Church on Saturday afternoon and Sunday. In the peak 53 cars left in one hour.

Southwark Street and London Bridge (Borough) Terminus

Southwark Street was cut through slums in 1865. It contained among the best commercial buildings of any street served by trams. The terminus was at the Hop Exchange: the cast-iron façade extends 200yd eastward from the railway bridge.

Route 12, sharing the terminus with route 26, formed a connecting line across all incoming routes except 70. After closure of routes 12 and 26, Southwark Street and Borough terminus were served for a further nine months by an extension of the 72 from Savoy Street.

Waterloo Station Terminus

Waterloo station was served by route 68, which united at Tower Bridge with the 70 from London Bridge to serve the dockland route to Greenwich. The terminus was in Waterloo Road north of The Cut at the now vanished Peartree Street. A grand landmark at the terminus was the since demolished Union Jack Club.

The Old Vic was damaged in the war. The November 1950 reopening ceremony, shown on television, also included a brief view of a 68 tram.

Blackfriars Road

Some interesting commercial buildings remain in Blackfriars Road. On the west side near St George's Circus is an extensive Peabody Trust estate.

Trams were delayed 25min from 8.15am on 12 June 1947, when a cable burned out at the Stamford Street points.

On 28 September 1950 a route 26 car derailed at Stamford Street at 8.09am: a gang had cleared the track 14min later!

Accidents at Christchurch, Lambeth

Five passengers were injured at Christchurch on 7 June 1950, when a route 35 car to Highgate and a 38 to Abbey Wood collided, delaying trams for 50min.

Trams and buses were halted for two hours at Christchurch on the evening of 26 August 1951, when a Peckham Rye-bound route 56 tram collided with a bus on route 153. Ten tram passengers suffered from shock, and 22 bus passengers were injured. It was believed the tram took the wrong path at the points. Crowds leaving Lambeth North station scattered as the tram lurched across the road.

Kennington Road

Laid out in the 1750s, Kennington Road still has fine terraces on the east side north of Kennington Lane. Since the days of the trams much improved, Kennington Road is quiet by today's standards, with 1,000 vehicles an hour in one direction in the peak.

After the war, the run-down Kennington Road had some of the worst track on the system. Between March and December 1949 gangs were busy tightening joints and relaying between Lambeth Road and The Horns tavern.

Kennington

When a route 18 tram stopped at Kennington Underground station at 10.20am on 24 August 1945, passengers heard screams, and saw the conductress bleeding from head wounds. Police questioned a woman passenger.

A 64-year old woman alighting from a tram at Kennington on 14 August 1949 was killed by a motorist who did not stop, but he was caught by another motorist at Balham.

Above and left:
21 July 1951: Newington Causeway just north of the Elephant and Castle, flanked by bombed sites in depth, view towards St George's church. 'HR/2' car No 157 on route 62 is bound for Southwark Bridge in the evening peak.

7 September 1986: A bus on route 133, in effect today's replacement for the route 10 tram.

Right and below:

30 December 1950: Only one week before closure of this tramway, 'Feltham' car No 2126 passes the London Fire Brigade Headquarters on the Albert Embankment at Black Prince Road. View towards Westminster. After regular services ceased the track remained and was used by at least one enthusiasts' special.

18 October 1987: Among demolitions on the Albert Embankment was the ornate Doulton Building (out of sight on the right) destroyed in the 1950s when the firm closed down. Dominating the foreground remains the headquarters of the London Fire Brigade, but beyond, the offices of W. H. Smith (with the tower) have gone.

Left and below left:
**8 September 1951:
Blackfriars Bridge from the
south, with 'HR/2' car
No 139. Note off-centre
conduit and police notices
reserving tracks on the west
side. The bridge was opened
in 1869 and widened in 1907-
10, increasing its overall
width from 70ft to 105ft. It is
still the widest Thames
bridge and wider than
Blackfriars Road.
Northbound traffic had to
cross both tracks south of the
bridge, causing confusion in
the morning peak.**

**28 November 1987: A bus on
route 63 heads south over the
bridge.**

At the Southwark inquest on the 22nd, a tram inspector and witnesses testified that the car knocked the woman the length of the tram. But the coroner claimed that there was no evidence of culpable negligence, and returned a verdict of accidental death!

Splayed Tracks in Inner South London

At some places on the Inner South London system, tracks were further apart than usual:

Westminster Bridge Road, between the railway bridge and Christchurch;

Lambeth Road, east of Kennington Road, and at the railway bridge;

North and south of The Cut in Waterloo Road;

Borough Road, at St George's Circus and Newington Causeway;

Southwark Street, junction of Blackfriars Road, and near Borough terminus;

Newington Causeway, north of the Elephant and Castle;

St George's Church, tracks from Marshalsea Road into Great Dover Street, and sharp curves from the latter into Borough High Street;

St George's Road, Elephant and Castle;

St George's Circus, east-to-west tracks;

Southwark Street, both sides of the junction with Southwark Bridge Road.

There was off-centre conduit on Blackfriars Bridge, in Westminster Bridge Road near County Hall, and even more pronounced on Southwark Bridge.

Large central islands were often sites for public conveniences, none of which now remains.

Above and above right:

24 February 1952: Westminster Bridge Road at Kennington Road, viewed towards Westminster from Christchurch, Lambeth, with 'E/3' car.

31 August 1986: The Lambeth Building Society has moved from the east to the west side of realigned Baylis Road.

Right and below right:

2 September 1950: Lambeth Road at Kennington Road, viewed towards St George's Circus, with an 'E/3' car. Westminster-bound trams could be diverted via Lambeth Road and Blackfriars, using the south-to-east curve from Kennington Road into Lambeth Road; the curve was disconnected in January 1951.

17 October 1987: DMS 2454 on route 44 replacing the 12 tram route, on the morning after the hurricane – an event evinced by the damaged trees in the background.

9

Wandsworth and Clapham Junction

The Vauxhall One-Way System

On the west side, the northbound track doubled before the junction, giving cars for Victoria and Westminster separate paths in advance of police-operated lights at Bridge-foot. Cars for Westminster had a central loading island.

Inward-bound cars could not reverse on the layout. In August 1950 some new conduit work was laid at facing points at the west end of Parry Street. This was used only until the end of September.

Nine Elms-Latchmere Hotel

In Nine Elms Lane, near Wandsworth Road, trams passed over level crossings of three and two railway tracks respectively, sidings in connection with Nine Elms Yard (itself since closed). On the north side approaching Battersea Park station was the large South Lambeth Goods Depot, demolished in 1988.

At the Latchmere Hotel were traces of east-to-north curves; here route 34 branched off along Battersea Park Road. There was a loading island for Blackfriars-bound route 34 cars in Battersea Bridge Road opposite the Latchmere.

Battersea Bridge and Kings Road Terminus

On the west side south of Battersea Bridge was a disused permanent way yard, with disconnected connection; the site is today occupied by housing.

Battersea Bridge, opened in 1890, with a 28ft-roadway, was the narrowest Thames bridge crossed by trams after the war. The two ramps lead up to a vaulted central arch. The tracks were laid at the kerb at each side of the bridge. The quiet terminus was in Beaufort Street at Kings Road.

On 26 March 1949 Clapham-bound 'E/1' car No 1597 and a petrol tanker collided on the north side of Battersea Bridge. Both caught fire; the tanker driver was badly injured, and the front of the tram damaged by fire, but it returned to service about six weeks later.

Wandsworth Depot and Wandsworth High Street Terminus

Beyond Princes Head, there was single track with two conduits in York Road east of Baldric Road, and a similar section west of Wandsworth Town station.

At Jews Row, east of Wandsworth Town station, the exit track from Wandsworth depot trailed on to the westbound in York Road. Wandsworth garage, closed in July 1987, is still used by London Coaches.

A roundabout at the south end of Wandsworth Bridge straddles the site of York Road. Beyond the railway bridge, as far as Morie Street, traffic is now diverted from the narrowed road. The last half mile as far as the former Wandsworth terminus is not served by buses.

Wandsworth High Street terminus, actually 150yd short thereof, was in York Road at Shoreham Street: double track continued beyond.

Top and above:
25 September 1950: The double track terminus of routes 26 and 28 at Clapham Junction was in St John's Hill at Severus Road, outside the Imperial Cinema. 'E/3' car No 210 is about to leave, and 'E/1' No 1824 waits to enter the terminus, which closed five days later.

27 April 1987: DMS2520 on route 77A passes the site of the former Imperial Cinema, but a great deal of the street scene remains otherwise unchanged.

Above and below:

28 September 1950: Falcon Road at Grant Road, viewed towards Clapham Junction, with 'E/1' car No 598 approaching Battersea, Princes Head, two days before closure of route 34. Trolleybus routes 626, 628, and 655 used St John's Hill and Falcon Road to reach their turning circle at this point.

27 April 1987: M964 on route 45 replacing the 34 tram route. The railway bridge has been cleaned up and repainted – presumably BR feels that it does not need to advertise its frequent services – and the pub has gained a new inn sign. It remains a Truman's house though.

Accidents at the Cedars Road/Lavender Hill Junction

Cedars Road descended continually from Clapham Common North Side, steepening to 1:15 150yd from the junction, where the tracks levelled out.

In July 1946 an 'E/1' car ran away on Cedars Road and overturned into Queenstown Road. Injured passengers, some thrown through the windows, were removed by three ambulances.

On 23 August 1950 rebuilt 'E/1' car No 1396, crowded on an early route 34 run to Battersea Bridge, derailed on the first part of the Cedars Road/Lavender Hill curve. It wrecked Hemming's corner baker shop. The injured driver was trapped, two passengers were hurt, and badly damaged No 1396 had to be withdrawn.

Cedars Road to Clapham Junction

From the top of Lavender Hill, there was a quarter-mile descent to Clapham Junction, where route 34 tracks passed on each side of a large island at the end of Falcon Road. Here were disconnected west-to-north curves from St John's Hill into Falcon Road.

On 20 May 1947 two buses and a tram collided in St John's Hill, injuring 27; the tram prevented a badly-damaged bus from overturning!

Car Types and Depot Allocation

When Wandsworth depot was equipped with overhead to facilitate rebuilding, the trams shed and received ploughs in Jews Row. It was the only south side depot with both trams and trolleybuses.

Cars on routes 12 and 31 were based at Wandsworth, which in September 1950 held 37 trams, all 'E/3s'. Routes 12 and 31 were normally worked by 'E/3s', but on 23 May 1949 an 'E/1' ran on route 12. Wandsworth and Clapham shared route 26, but Clapham provided all route 28 cars.

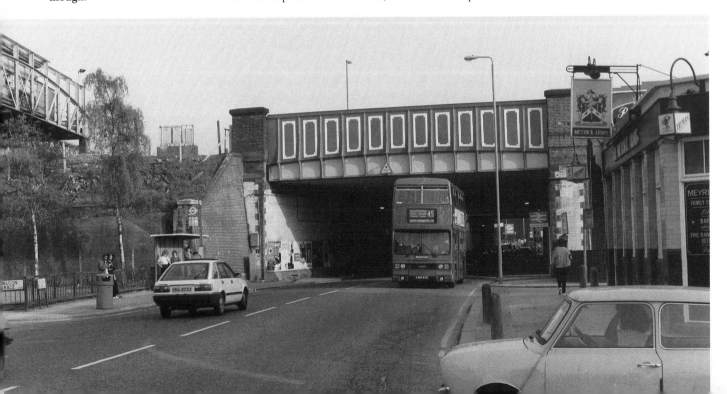

In June 1949 route 34 workings went from Clapham to Camberwell depot; thereafter, 'HR/2', 'E/3' and 'E/1' cars, including streamlined car No 1103, ran on route 34.

The Replacing Routes Today

Bus route 44 replaces tram route 12 and trolleybus route 612. Bus routes 45 and 45A cover the 34 tram, with an overlap between Brixton and the Elephant and Castle.

Bus route 170 replacing the 31 tram runs to Aldwych from Monday to Friday, but on Saturday only to Vauxhall; it runs via Clapham Junction, avoiding York Road. The successor to the 26 and 28 trams is the 156 bus, from Clapham Junction to Vauxhall, Monday-Friday peak hours only. All-night tram route 3, Battersea, Princes Head-Blackfriars, is covered by bus route N83; and all-night tram route 26, by bus route N68.

Passengers could use route 26 cars on Wandsworth depot runs. Today, buses running to off-route garages often run empty.

Above left and left:
28 September 1950: Battersea Park Road, from the bottom of Falcon Road (in the right foreground), viewed towards Vauxhall. Note the loading island and temporary stop sign. Two days later, these tracks served by routes 12, 31 and 34 were abandoned. Trolleybus route 612 terminated in a clockwise loop round the green in the background, returning along York Road to Mitcham.

11 July 1987: A bus on route 44, replacing both the 12 tram and the 612 trolleybus routes.

10

Clapham, Tooting and Wimbledon

The Horns, Kennington

The Kennington Road/Kennington Park Road junction was known to tramwaymen as The Horns, a public house at the northwest corner. An office block has replaced The Horns and the ruined Assembly Rooms. The tram tracks here passed on each side of a large island.

Kennington Common and Kennington Gate

Parts of Kennington Common were given up in the early 19th century for building Camberwell New Road, and for St Mark's church. Before 1852, the junction of the Brixton and Clapham Roads was further north, towards The Horns. To avoid infringing the Park, a new junction was made to the south: the resited toll gate was removed in 1865. The term Kennington Gate, current in tram days, is no longer in use.

A 40min delay occurred at Kennington Gate on 7 May 1948, while a crew worked to fit a spare plough.

Stockwell

Most of the property on the wide road from the Oval to Union Road, Clapham, consisted of Regency and Victorian houses; much has since gone. At Stockwell station there was a loading island for northbound cars. Adjacent to the war memorial in the centre of the roundabout is a ventilation shaft for the Northern Line duplicate tunnels.

In the gutter at the end of Binfield Road, north of Stockwell station, one can still see slots where point levers were inserted.

Vauxhall to Brixton via Stockwell

South Lambeth Road was served at all times by routes 8 and 20; on weekdays only by route 78; and in the peak also by routes 22 and 24. Sections of the northbound track were relaid in August and September 1949; in February 1950, parts of Stockwell junction were renewed.

The driver of a flour lorry was badly injured when he collided with 'Feltham' car No 2097 on route 20 in South Lambeth Road on 10 May 1948. The tram ended up in a front garden.

In Stockwell Road there was single track with two conduits between Rumsey Road and Moat Place: between these streets, horse tram track still remains in an entry. Parts of both Stockwell Road tracks were relaid in August 1950.

Above left and left:

25 September 1950: The Swan, Stockwell, viewed towards Brixton, during the last week of route 34. 'E/3' car No 1933 turns from Stockwell Road into Clapham Road. There was a curious kink in the southbound track south of the junction, possibly to ease this curve.

16 August 1986: T1049 on route 45 replacing the 34 tram route. Remarkably, all the buildings have survived, although the scene is cluttered with modern street furniture.

Clapham Road and Clapham High Street

Returning a verdict of accidental death on 21 January 1949 at the Southwark inquest on an elderly woman killed near a pedestrian crossing in Clapham Road, the jury added that the tram driver should have taken more care. The driver stated that the woman hesitated, then rushed in front of the tram, which was hard to stop on greasy rails.

Joints on the southbound track in Clapham High Street as far as Clapham Manor Street were attended to in August 1949; the work was repeated in September 1950.

Clapham Depot and Clapham Common Station

Opposite the closed Majestic Cinema was the entrance to Clapham depot, the tracks making trailing junctions with the line in High Street. A single exit line left the rear of the depot, where war damage was still visible, by Triangle Place and Clapham Park Road, and trailed on to each track at Clapham Common station. Thus cars entering had to reverse, but those leaving had a clear run north or south.

'Felthams' were not based on Clapham depot, but on occasion, eg on 15 August and 11 November 1950, entered from the High Street.

At Clapham Common station there was a lengthy southbound loading island at the Long Road traffic lights; northbound cars stopped at the Underground station.

The Clapham Common Turning Circle

When two trams collided at Clapham Common South Side, in October 1948, the conductor of the first and stationary car, who was on the top deck, received fatal injuries. The driver of the second car said that as he was crossing the facing points at The Avenue, he applied the magnetic brake, but to no effect; the rails were greasy with wet leaves, and collision occurred at 6mph. It was reported on 12 June 1950 that the conductor's widow was to receive £2,540 from London Transport in settlement of an action in the King's Bench Division.

The turning circle where the accident occurred was used by learner cars after the war; it was disconnected in March 1949.

The Tramcar Film Studio

At Clapham South there was a loading island for southbound cars. The crossover had unexpected use: for two hours on 13 March 1948 Richard Attenborough rode up and down in a tram between here and the Bedford Hill facing crossover, near Balham station, making a scene for *London Belongs to Me*. The Odeon Cinema near Clapham South station had been renamed Carlton. The tramcar scenes were cut from the finished film, but the Odeon still exists, though rebuilt.

Balham High Road

On 4 January 1951 a tram, believed to have been 'E/1' car No 1312 on tow after a breakdown, caught fire in the Balham High Road and burned fiercely for 10min.

After heavy rain, trams caused a bow-wave at the dip under Balham station bridge. The southbound track south thereof was very bad: some relaying was done in March 1949.

Marius Road

The Marius Road crossover was sometimes used for short working: destination blinds bore this indication. Drivers often filled their tea cans at a nearby café: it was common to see a tram driving itself, while the driver drank tea, as the controller handle could be left untended on any power notch.

Also on the west side, at Marius Road, was a former depot, then used as a garage, but since demolished. At the end of 1949 deep excavations were made under the southbound track opposite the former depot; the T-rails were disconnected, trams coasting over the gap.

Tooting Broadway to St Leonard's Church

Cars on route 10, the only route using both west-to-east tracks at Tooting Broadway, terminated about 150yd west thereof.

Trams were delayed for 25min on the afternoon of 22 February 1947, while a second tram rerailed one that had derailed at Amen Corner. The busy shopping area east of Tooting is now very dingy and the road bears heavy traffic.

The curve from Mitcham Lane into Southcroft Road was on a falling gradient with adverse camber: a tram derailed here on 30 December 1947, causing a 20min delay.

Single track in Mitcham Lane, at Westcote Road, was followed by a hump-backed bridge and more single line at Fernwood Avenue by Streatham Green. Streatham High Road was joined at St Leonard's Church.

Longley Road Change-Pit

At the change-pit by picturesque Waterfall House, trams went on to the overhead system. From the London County Council boundary at Longley Road to Wimbledon was the last surviving tramway formerly worked by a company: the London United Tramways.

Short-working cars showing 'MERTON' reversed north of the change-pit, and there was another crossover just beyond, on the overhead section.

Colliers Wood

Half a mile beyond Longley Road, a ruined Toll House of the Surrey Iron Railway was passed: this relic has since been destroyed.

During a violent thunderstorm that broke just after nightfall on 19 September 1947 lightning struck a feeder pillar at Pincott

Road, Colliers Wood. The power failure halted trams between that point and Colliers Wood station for 30min.

On 7 December 1946 a lorry collided with a tram at High Street, Merton and derailed it, then rebounded into another lorry, which overturned. The tracks were blocked for 30min.

The Merton Road Single Track

At the end of the two single track sections in Merton Road, a semaphore light signal faced each double line; there were four signals in all, necessitated by blind corners at each end of the road. Even so, two Wimbledon-bound

Below and bottom:

18 November 1950: Merton Road from High Street Merton, viewed towards Wimbledon. 'E/1' car No 1836 is entering the single track. There was a sharp curve from High Street, Merton, into Merton Road, which had single track sections at each end, with a passing loop at Pelham Road. Cars entering Merton Road at South Wimbledon were often delayed by oncoming traffic.

5 March 1988: Despite the widened road, buses are still stranded in the traffic.

trams met one going the other way on the Pelham Road to Trinity Road single in fog of 20yd visibility on 26 November 1950.

Wimbledon

The middle of the road terminal layout was very convenient, and contrasts with today's dispersed bus stops. Hampton Court trolley-buses, terminating at the Town Hall, made a clockwise loop round the island.

Car Types and Depot Allocation

In May 1950, routes 2, 4 and 6, and some turns on routes 8 and 20 were based on Clapham depot, which held a maximum of 93 cars after the war. Clapham cars were mostly '1800' series 'E/1s', with some older 'E/1s': they were used indiscriminately on all services.

Operation of Routes 2 and 4

Route 2 was allowed 8min from Balham station to Clapham Common station; 18min to the Oval; 28min to Westminster; and 35min to Blackfriars (6½ miles). Route 4 cars were allowed 25min to the Elephant and Castle; and 35min to Blackfriars (5¾ miles).

The timing from Balham to the Elephant and Castle had been increased to 36min by 1991. The peak hour service on routes 2/4 was every 5min. Replacing buses 155 and 355 combined to give a 7½min interval between Colliers Wood and Stockwell, but south and north thereof, only 15min.

Fares and Replacing Buses

Fares between the Embankment and Wimbledon had doubled within 10 years of bus conversion. The single fare from Balham to the Embankment increased 60 times from 1945 to 1987, but in 1945 there were no ride-at-will tickets.

The sole remaining Clapham Road replacements are the 155 and 355 bus routes: the 155 runs daily from Wimbledon to Vauxhall; and the 355 from Colliers Wood to the Elephant and Castle (not Sundays). The peak hour extension of the 155 via the Elephant and Castle to Aldwych ceased at the end of 1987.

The route 10 tram is now covered by bus 133 between Borough station and Tooting Broadway, but the former bus 95 replacement now runs to Streatham Garage.

With cessation of buses replacing tram routes 6, 8, 20, 22 and 24, Clapham and Tooting are hard hit. Loss of the Tooting and Streatham circulars to Victoria and the Embankment means that the Southcroft Road/Mitcham Lane area is worse served.

All-night route 1, Tooting and Streatham circular, is represented today by bus route N78 to Streatham; route N87 to Tooting and terminating at St Leonard's Church is the last relic of the former Tooting and Streatham circulars.

Left and below:

19 November 1950: Wimbledon terminus at the Town Hall, showing the only scissors crossover on the postwar system, and 'E/1' cars Nos **1838** and **1841**. The trolley pole of No **1841** is being lowered. It was the only terminus where cars loaded side by side. On the right is a trolleybus for Hampton Court.

23 August 1986: A bus passes on route 57. Note that the modern No Entry signs reuse the columns for **40** years earlier.

The Croydon Routes

Kennington-Brixton

On the west side of Brixton Road, near Camberwell New Road, the Cable Tea Rooms marks the northern cable car terminus. There are fine terraces near Vassall Road, and north of Gresham Road, but much of elegant Angell Town has been demolished.

A remarkable number of mishaps occurred in Brixton Road in latter years. Trams were often diverted via Stockwell Road and Clapham Road, involving shunting at Stockwell — unthinkable today!

Spectacular Derailments at Brixton

Pedestrians scattered on 19 May 1950 when a route 78 tram derailed at the Stockwell Road/Brixton Road junction. It came to a rest at the kerb, causing a 23min delay.

In a similar mishap there on 14 August 1950 shoppers are reported to have screamed as a tram on route 78 took the curve from Stockwell Road into Brixton Road too fast, and ran off the rails. Careering towards the pavement, it jarred to a halt at the kerb, injuring two pedestrians.

The Centre of Brixton

Whereas in tram days there was a simple bifurcation at Lambeth Town Hall, today St Mark's Church is the focus of a noisy roundabout. Traffic levels are high at all hours. The Victoria Line has not arrested Brixton's decline.

Over 500 children, invited by porters and staff of Borough Market, rode on five trams to a matinee of *Babes in the Wood* at the Brixton Empress on 3 January 1950.

The southbound track in Brixton Road between Gresham Road and the railway bridges was relaid in February 1951. Worn out track at the southbound Acre Lane loading island had been renewed in February

1949. At the Town Hall was an island for northbound cars.

Brixton Hill

From Brixton to near Christchurch Road was a one-mile continuous climb, the longest on the postwar system: it sorely taxed the 'Felthams'. Old houses in extensive gardens have mostly given way to flats.

Brixton Hill Depot

Brixton Hill depot was on the east side of the road just north of Christchurch Road. The shed was equipped with overhead and there were two change-pits in the entrance. The exit tracks made trailing connections with both tracks in Brixton Hill. The depot was an annexe to Telford Avenue.

The building still exists, the ornamental cornice bearing the date 1923. In the fore-court is evidence of conduit track, slot rail and wood blocks.

Telford Avenue Depot

A quarter-mile beyond on the same side, past Pullman Court, Telford Avenue depot consisted of two sheds separated by a Water Board main. The still-existing reservoir was located to the east of the depot. From Streatham Hill, ramps led up to both sheds. The northern shed exit tracks trailed on to both tracks in the road; the southern shed had a trailing connection with the south-bound track.

A mechanical defect at Telford Avenue depot, probably breakdown of the traverser, delayed trams leaving on 11 April 1947. Trams were again late leaving the depot on the morning of 7 June 1950, due to traverser trouble.

Streatham High Road

The narrow road at Streatham Hill station caused regular traffic jams: when a tram fouled the points here on 3 December 1947, a delay of 83min resulted. In the very wide road beyond trams had the central strip to themselves.

Passengers had to leave a route 16 tram in Streatham High Road on 29 September 1948, due to smoke caused by a fused switch. On 1 February 1949 a tram caught fire in Streatham High Road.

St Leonard's Church and Streatham Change-Pit

Passengers on a route 16 tram at St Leonard's Church broke upper deck windows on 9 February 1950, when a fuse caused dense smoke. Current was cut off on both tracks for at least 20min.

The pointsman at St Leonard's Church, who claimed to be the last former horse tram driver, retired on 20 January 1948 aged 70.

Below left and below:
29 December 1951: An 'E/3' car turns from Stockwell Road into Brixton Road only six days before route 78 ceased operation, in a view looking north. At Brixton route 34 crossed from Stockwell Road into Gresham Road, where there was a change-pit outside the police station.

10 April 1988: Since 1951 the bomb-damaged shop has been repaired and, whilst the majority of buildings remain intact, the spire of the Congregational Church has been dismantled leaving the stump of a tower.

Once Mr Albert Humphries inadvertently held up Queen Victoria's carriage with his tram in Camberwell New Road. He drove the first car from Streatham to Blackfriars in 1904, and in 1919 became points inspector.

Trams for Croydon descended sharply beyond St Leonard's, falling rapidly below the level of those to Tooting at Streatham Green. At the foot of the hill trams changed over to overhead at Gleneagle Road; it was the only change-pit on a busy main road.

The County Boundary at Norbury

At the S-curve at Hermitage Bridge, Nor-bury, where trams passed from London into Surrey, peak hour extras reversed on a facing crossover. The line southwards was the only part of the postwar system formerly worked by an outer London municipality, in this case Croydon Corporation. Until April 1951, ex-Croydon cars ran only on routes 16, 18 and 42.

The Thornton Heath Branch

At the junction beyond the now filled-in Thornton Heath pond, the mile-long Thornton Heath branch diverged to the east along Brigstock Road. For almost a half-mile

Right and below right:
24 March 1951: 'E/3' car No 1907 on interlaced track in Brigstock Road at Brook Road, viewed towards Thornton Heath terminus. The use of bracket arms was unusual on the postwar system. There was always a separate overhead wire for each direction.

28 April 1990: DMS2320 on route 250 replacing the 42 tram route. Although the scene is dominated by the office block in the background, the low rise buildings in the foreground survive from an earlier age.

Far right, top and bottom:
25 March 1951: North End at George Street viewed towards Thornton Heath Pond. A 'Feltham' car bound for Purley is entering the single track. At the Whitgift Almshouses, on the right, the narrow road necessitated single track with semaphore light signals. Here trams often had to wait for each other.

26 July 1987: The west side of the road has since been widened, although both the 16th century Whitgift Almshouses and the Allders department store remain.

72

15 January 1950: Purley depot on the east side of Brighton Road, just south of the Royal Oak at Riddlesdown Road, with ex-Croydon car No 384. The two staggered sheds unusually had two exit tracks each trailing on to the northbound track in Brighton Road. Only two weeks earlier, the depot had been reopened as a running shed.

29 September 1988: Forty years on and whilst the building remains recognisable its use has dramatically changed. Where trams were once maintained, shoppers now buy their household goods and gardening equipment.

beyond Frant Road, the line was single, with short loops at Colliers Water Lane and Chipstead Avenue, and a third west of Thornton Heath station. The last loop ended in interlaced track. There was a final single track section just north of Whitehorse Lane, before the terminus in Whitehorse Road at Talbot Road.

Route 42 had a 3min interval in the peak and on Saturday afternoons; on occasion, extras were run.

Thornton Heath Depot

Thornton Heath depot was just south of Brigstock Road, on the west side of London Road; the connecting track trailed on to the northbound in London Road, just north of the Brigstock Road junction. Let into the depot frontage was a World War 1 memorial tablet to Croydon tramwaymen.

Central Croydon

In Croydon there are still many Croydon Corporation Tramways inspection covers in the footways.

On 29 May 1947, 13 people were hurt when a tram collided with a lorry in London Road.

South Croydon

Route 42 terminated in South End at Parker Road, cars laying over on the southbound track until a Purley-bound car came. After the war, indicators of southbound route 42 cars showed 'GREYHOUND', but latterly 'CROYDON' instead.

Depot Allocation and Car Types

Route 42 was worked by 'E/3' and ex-Croydon cars, from Thornton Heath depot until the end of 1949, and from Purley depot thereafter. At midnight on 1 January 1950 all Thornton Heath cars moved to Purley. In September 1950, Purley accommodated 32 cars, nine of them 'E/3s', the rest ex-Croydon cars. Purley worked some turns on routes 16 and 18.

In May 1950, Telford Avenue and Brixton Hill depots provided all cars for routes 22 and 24; most on routes 8 and 20; and about three-quarters of those for routes 16 and 18. Route 10 working was shared with Norwood depot.

Routes 16 and 18 were worked by 'Feltham', ex-Walthamstow, ex-Croydon and 'E/3' cars. Latterly the proportion of 'E/3s' on Telford Avenue routes rose due to the progressive withdrawal of 'Felthams' for Leeds. Some 'Felthams' were running until the end of the Croydon routes in April 1951. Routes 8 and 20 were worked towards the end by 'Felthams' and 'E/3s'; and routes 22 and 24 by 'E/3s' with the occasional 'Feltham'.

Car No 1

Always well maintained, car No 1 ran from Telford Avenue until the end of the Croydon routes. It normally worked peak hour extras from the Embankment to Norbury: the seven-miles run from Blackfriars to Streatham could take as much as 46min.

From February 1950 car No 1 was occasionally seen on normal workings: on the 18th it was on route 20; and from June sometimes on route 24 in the morning peak.

Operation of the Croydon Routes and Fast Runs

Although 37min were allowed from St Leonard's to Purley this was often much reduced. On 1 April 1951 'Feltham' car No 2160 ran the 12½ miles from Purley to Charing Cross via Westminster in 64½min, 13½min less than scheduled, at an average of 11.62mph. From Purley to St Leonard's took 32½min.

The fastest run experienced on routes 16/18 was on 'E/3' car No 1913 on 11 March 1951. The 11¼ miles from Purley to the Elephant and Castle were covered in 55min, an average of 12.27mph; 2½min were clipped from the previously noticed run between Purley and the Oval.

The three miles between Purley and West Croydon station regularly took 12min or less. Of the 11 stops from Purley to Surrey Street, Croydon, only three were compulsory.

The weekday peak hour timing from West Croydon station to Westminster was 50min, against 64min for today's buses; from St Leonard's to Westminster, trams were allowed 30min, but buses now take 42min.

Replacing Bus Routes

Bus route 109, in place of the 16 and 18 trams, runs from Croydon High Street to Trafalgar Square, from Monday to Friday only. Purley-Blackfriars is covered by bus route 59 from Monday to Friday; on Saturday the route ends at Brixton. Tram route 42 from Thornton Heath to Central Croydon is covered by bus routes 119, 194B and 250.

Herne Hill and Loughborough Junction

18 September 1950: At the change-pit in Gresham Road at the junction with Brixton Road 'E/3' car No 192 takes up the plough.

22 April 1987: T1039 on route 45 replacing the 34 tram route; the police station has since been rebuilt.

A Small Overhead Wire Network

The mileage of this group of routes was 4½; it was bounded by Brixton, Camberwell and West Norwood. Change-pits were in Coldharbour Lane at Denmark Hill; Effra Road, Brixton; and Gresham Road, Brixton.

Gresham Road and Coldharbour Lane

There was a left-hand turn from Gresham Road into Coldharbour Lane and single track at Belinda Street, where the first of three railway bridges crossed the still-narrow road.

Two people were injured on 30 December 1949 when a tram, a lorry and a bus collided in Coldharbour Lane. The lorry and tram were badly damaged. The driver of the route 34 tram was also injured. The tram, believed to have been car No 1103, was later repaired to run for a further two years.

The Curious Layout at Loughborough Junction

Route 48 cars bound for West Norwood crossed to the wrong track, using a facing crossover under the northern railway bridge, turning south into Herne Hill Road along single track. This curve was latterly protected by semaphore light signals removed from Merton Road, Wimbledon. In Coldharbour Lane there were fossilised west-to-south curves.

One-Way Tracks South of Loughborough Junction

South of the single track was a section of double. After right- and left-hand curves, there was once again single track. Then the southbound followed Poplar Walk Road (now Poplar Road) and Lowden Road; and the northbound Milkwood Road.

Where the routes rejoined, one-third of a mile north of Herne Hill, was a crossover. Trams passed the station platforms on the level, but descended sharply beyond to turn right under the railway bridge, joining the route to Brixton at the entrance to Brockwell Park. Northbound cars followed the railway viaduct most of the way. The Herne Hill to Loughborough Junction route lay along quiet residential roads.

Norwood Depot and Norwood Terminus

The depot was in Norwood Road south of Elmcourt Road. Both exit tracks joined the northbound in Norwood Road, with facing and trailing junctions respectively when going north. After passing through the entrance archway, two tracks led to the depot, which lay well back from the road and consisted of three bays.

The largely unaltered shed is presently used by Howard Smith Paper. The archway with offices above is still in situ. Opposite the old depot is the Electric Café.

At 6.27am on 1 May 1951 a lorry skidded into a tram standard outside the depot and burst into flames. Fire engines from the sta-

Left and below:

18 September 1950: Denmark Hill from Coldharbour Lane, viewed towards Camberwell Green, with 'E/1' car No 592; the standard in the centre anchors the end of the Coldharbour Lane overhead. Just south of Denmark Hill, route 34 cars changed back to conduit; it was the only postwar route to pass two change-pits.

7 September 1986: A bus on route 35 passes the still extant shopping parade. In amongst the Indian restaurants and the picture gallery, the outfitters George Selman remain a permanent fixture.

tion next door blocked the depot entrance, delaying trams for 16min.

The terminus was before the church of St Luke, which has the finest site of any Waterloo church. The terminal layout consisted of 100yd of single track ending in Norwood High Street on the east side of the churchyard. Cars waiting to occupy the terminus stood at Robson Road.

Herne Hill to Brixton

At the Herne Hill entrance to Brockwell Park, a London County Council section box bears the inscription 'L.C.C. TRAMWAYS 1917', where trams once diverged northwest to Brixton.

The change-pit on to the conduit system in Effra Road was just south of Lambeth Town Hall, at St Matthew's churchyard.

Car Types and Depot Allocation

Normally 'E/3s' were used on routes 33, 48 and 78, but route 48 was sometimes worked by rebuilt 'E/1s'. In September 1950 there were 61 cars at Norwood depot: it worked all cars on routes 48 and 78, and some on routes 10 and 33. Norwood's rebuilt 'E/1s' in the '1300' and '1500' series were badly maintained.

Replacing Bus Routes

Route 33 ran daily; route 48 was curtailed at St George's Church on Saturday afternoon and Sunday; and route 78 ran weekdays only.

The area between Herne Hill and Loughborough Junction has no bus service today. Bus route 68 serves much of the course of tram route 48 south of the Elephant and Castle, running more to the east between Denmark Hill and Herne Hill.

Bus route 2 covers most of the 78 tram route, but follows a different course between Herne Hill and Brixton. Bus route 3 serves the Lambeth Road-Herne Hill section of tram route 33.

Above and left:

16 March 1952: '**E/3**' **car No 1956 skirts Brockwell Park in Norwood Road at Rosendale Road, viewed north towards Herne Hill. The double track south of Herne Hill was on the west side of Norwood Road, alongside Brockwell Park, and was an arrangement much criticised.**

5 November 1988: A bus passes on route 2.

16 March 1952: Brixton
Water Lane at Trelawn Road,
viewed towards Brixton, with
'E/3' car No 1997. Half a mile
north of Herne Hill was a
one-way system, which saw
southbound cars using
Morval Road, and
northbound cars Brixton
Water Lane.

19 December 1986: A bus on
route 3 approaches along
Dalberg Road.

13

The Dog Kennel Hill Routes

Walworth Road

As the route from Camberwell Green to Forest Hill had steep gradients, 'HR/2' cars were used on routes 56, 58, 60, 62 and 84: all but route 58 ran via Walworth Road. Tram traffic to East Street market on Sundays was heavy. Passengers could carry bulky items on the front platform of trams; today luggage is unsupervised and carried at the bus driver's discretion only.

Camberwell Depot

At each entrance, in Camberwell Green and Camberwell New Road, depot connections trailed on to each street track. The track connection between the two sheds was unsuitable for general use.

In May 1950, stock consisted of 143 cars: 87 'HR/2s'; 34 'E/3s'; and 22 'E/1s' of various types. Routes 34, 56, 58, 60, 62 and 84 ran from Camberwell depot, as did some cars on route 35. Camberwell was second only to New Cross in the number of trams operated.

Camberwell lost its 'E/1s' when route 34 closed in September 1950. Walworth bus garage on the site closed in November 1985, but reopened in 1988 for Red Arrow buses.

Camberwell Green

The Camberwell Green crossing had north-to-east and west-to-south double track connections. One could stand on the large island southeast of the junction and watch trams pass at the rate of 250 an hour. The duty regulator stood in the road unhindered by traffic. Delays in crew-changing prompted a press complaint on 14 January 1949 that six trams at a time were held up.

Above right and right:

9 September 1951: 'HR/2' car No 107 enters Camberwell depot from Camberwell Green; by the entrance is the 'BEWARE CARS CROSSING' sign. Camberwell depot, consisting of two sheds, had entrances in Camberwell New Road and in Camberwell Green, the former 200yd from the junction, and the latter 150yd. Since most depot connections trailed on to street tracks, cars usually had to reverse to enter.

17 August 1986: A disused entrance to Walworth garage is beside the first building. Part of the depot now forms the car park for a Queensway store.

Denmark Hill

At the junction of Coldharbour Lane was the only set of automatic conduit points on the system; application of power altered the points, but cars coasted if they were correctly set. All points at busy junctions were manned; the often elderly pointsmen were provided with little huts for shelter.

There were 30min delays on 7 November 1947 and on 30 May 1950 when derailments occurred at the Coldharbour Lane junction, where the Odeon Cinema has long been derelict.

Southwards, the climbing started. Past King's College Hospital, a left-hand curve led into Champion Park, vaulted by tall trees. In October 1950 the outer curve was relaid

Above and right:

23 September 1951: Dog Kennel Hill at Albrighton Road, viewed towards Forest Hill, with 'HR/2' car No 1894. The outside tracks branched off as turnouts at Grove Hill Road, just below the summit, but the trailing junction of the southbound tracks at Quorn Road, at the bottom, was parallel. Latterly the middle tracks were the most used.

1 February 1987: A route 184 bus replacing the 56/84 tram routes.

Far right, top and bottom:

29 July 1951: Approaching Peckham Rye terminus, a route 56 car runs beside Peckham Rye Common seen looking north.

24 April 1988: Forty years on and little has changed. The road has been resurfaced and the fences have either been replaced or removed.

along with the westbound track in Champion Park.

Dog Kennel Hill

A right-hand curve and sharp climb up Grove Lane, passing prefabricated houses on the left, brought trams to the top of Dog Kennel Hill: a fine view across Dulwich.

The 440yd-long, 1:10 gradient of Dog Kennel Hill was laid with four tracks, allowing two cars to ascend or descend at the same time. The very wide roadway narrowed at Quorn Road. In June 1951 parts of both downhill tracks, and sections of both at the top of the hill, were relaid.

The Peckham Rye Branch

After a reverse curve through Grove Vale, the Peckham Rye branch diverged at the site of today's Goose Green roundabout. Trailing points of the disued east-to-south connecting curve were renewed in April 1951.

On 28 March 1950 five people were hurt when two trams collided at Goose Green. Passengers were thrown to the floor, broken glass covered the road, and road blocks were torn up. Nearby residents took shocked passengers into their houses.

The Peckham Rye branch was one mile long. For the last half mile it followed the west side of the road beside Peckham Rye Park, giving kerbside loading for Embankment-bound trams.

At the junction of East Dulwich Road and Peckham Rye, the line passed close to Rye Lane Permanent Way Yard. From this depot, without track connection, the South London tracks were maintained.

The Climb Through Dulwich to Horniman's Museum

The line through Dulwich to Forest Hill along pleasant residential roads climbed steadily to a summit at Horniman's Gardens; it was still sett-paved from Court Lane southwards. On the long descent to Goose Green 'HR/2' cars showed their free-running and steady riding qualities.

At Dulwich Common, the South Circular joins Lordship Lane, and was followed by the 58 tram route to Rushey Green. In 1977, parts of the South Circular carried 36,000 vehicles daily.

Peak hour route 60 from Southwark Bridge terminated at Dulwich Library. In October 1949, track was being relaid at points between Goose Green and Forest Hill. In October/November 1950, much of both tracks between East Dulwich station and Forest Hill was renewed.

Forest Hill

There was a sharp descent to Forest Hill station past Victorian villas, those on the south side having given way to blocks of flats. At the station, trams curved sharply to the left, then a continual right-hand curve brought the line to a junction with the terminal stub of routes 35 and 66 in Waldram Park Road. Part of the Forest Hill station crossover was renewed in June 1951.

Operation

There was a 4 to 6min interval on route 58, which needed 24 cars even on Sundays. In the peak, 90 cars an hour used Dog Kennel Hill.

The fastest route 58 run was recorded on 10 May 1951, when the 8½ miles from Greenwich Church to the Oval were covered in 45½min, an average of 11.2mph; only 19min were taken from Forest Hill to the Oval.

Replacing Bus Services

Tram routes 56 and 84 are covered by bus route 184, Elephant and Castle-Lewisham, via Brockley; in the peak it is extended over Westminster Bridge, with some early morning journeys along the Embankment. Bus route 185 replacing tram route 58 runs as far as Lewisham only.

South of St George's Circus, tram route 62 is covered by bus route 176, Aldwych-Penge; this route also replaces tram route 60 south of the Elephant and Castle. The 185A bus route corresponds to the Saturday afternoon and evening working of the 62 tram route — Elephant and Castle-Lewisham — a remarkable survival. The Dulwich and Forest Hill areas have fared well in respect of tram replacements.

14

Victoria to Forest Hill via Brockley

Victoria Terminus

Mr Alfred Barnes, Minister of Transport, stated on 19 June 1946 that the tram terminus could not be improved, due to lack of space. Despite this, a new loading island came into use there on 3 August 1949. It was 80yd south of the existing refuge opposite the New Victoria Cinema, was 80ft long and nearly 6ft wide, and was built by Westminster Council in eight days.

Passengers for routes 54 and 58 boarded at the southern end and those for route 66 at the northern end. Routes 8 and 20 used the rear of the old island, and routes 28 and 78 the front end. In the evening peak about 7,800 passengers left on 87 trams, five loading at once.

Vauxhall Bridge Road and Vauxhall Bridge

Vauxhall Bridge Road narrowed progressively towards Rochester Row, but was adequate for the traffic of those days. A tram driver, conductress, and two passengers were injured on the north side of Vauxhall Bridge on 12 December 1945 when the brakes of a Victoria-bound route 54 car failed; it ran into a tram on route 20. The ends of both trams were badly damaged, and most windows broken.

Tram Conductor Killed in Vauxhall Bridge Road

At the Southward inquest on 29 August 1950 into an accident on the 23rd, a passenger on a route 54 tram said that he noticed the conductor leaning out from the front platform behind the driver. 'I think he was trying to do something . . . Another tram approached from the opposite direction, and there was a thud as it passed.'

The driver of the tram stated: 'Going along Vauxhall Bridge Road I heard a noise from the rear of my tram. My conductor came on to the front platform and said that a chain was hanging. I told him to wait until later before doing anything . . . I was concentrating on my driving . . . but he may have leant out to adjust the chain'.

The driver of the oncoming tram said he was doing 15mph and felt a bump on passing the car on route 54. The conductor died shortly after the accident from head injuries.

Vauxhall-the Oval

Oval-bound trams had a direct run into Harleyford Road at Vauxhall; those to Victoria passed round three sides of the roundabout.

The tramway skirted the south side of the Oval cricket ground, giving top deck passengers a good view. The volume of tram traffic fell by one-half towards the Oval, where there was a right-angled crossing at the Underground station. The line from Kennington joined at the Kennington Park entrance.

At the exit points from Camberwell New Road, northbound trams often cut across eastbound traffic, encouraged by lack of a green filter for northbound traffic. Given the rapid acceleration of trams, this led to several near misses between Embankment-bound trams and other traffic.

Camberwell New Road

A tram, private car, coach and taxi collided in Camberwell New Road at Wyndham Road on 25 June 1949. The wrecked car was wedged between coach and tram; both tracks were blocked for 24min.

The Camberwell New Road entrance to Camberwell depot was on the north side of the road, east of the railway bridge near Camberwell Green.

Peckham Road and Peckham High Street

Eight people were trapped on the top deck of a bus when its staircase was crushed in collision with a tram in Peckham Road on 8 November 1950. Most windows in the tram were broken.

During July 1950, much track was relaid in Peckham Road. Services were delayed on 17 September 1947 when a tram reversing at the Rye Lane crossover derailed, blocking both tracks; it was rerailed by two trams, one pushing and one pulling.

Between Peckham High Street and New Cross were many fine old houses; some villas remain on the south side, east of the railway bridge. The approach to New Cross has been opened out since the trams went, with a diversion into New Cross Road.

New Cross Gate

The north-to-west curves of the triangular junction at New Cross Gate were not regularly used. On 16 February 1951 'E/1' car No 1818 derailed when running into Queen's Road over the curve. Crossovers north and west of the junction were sprung on the Lon-

Far right, top and bottom:
18 August 1951: Vauxhall, Bridgefoot, viewed towards the Oval, with 'HR/2' car No 128; on the left is an 'E/3' on route 54. Vauxhall Bridge, opened in 1906, the second widest bridge used by trams, has a 70ft-roadway.

31 January 1987: On the left is an RM on route 36B replacing the 54 tram route; in front of it, an RML on route 88.

don side, to facilitate reversal of inward-bound trams.

Formerly in the centre of the junction, the underground toilets here, apparently in original state, were opened in 1897.

Eleven persons were injured on 25 September 1951, when a route 52 tram crashed into the rear of a car on route 40 at New Cross Gate. Among the injured were the driver and conductor of the second tram. The tracks were blocked by the badly damaged cars.

New Cross Depot

In September 1950, 254 trams were based at New Cross, the largest depot. Until abandonment started in October 1950, the stock had been entirely 'E/1' and rebuilt 'E/1' cars, apart from 'E/3' car No 164, based there at least since February 1949. During 1951, '1800' series 'E/1' ex-Croydon, ex-Walthamstow, 'E/3', and 'HR/2' cars replaced most of the older 'E/1s'.

New Cross supplied all cars for routes 40, 52, 54, 66, 68, 70, 72 and 74. Working of

routes 36, 38 and 46 was shared with Abbey Wood depot.

In November 1950, the western entrance curve into New Cross depot, and the parallel and trailing points in the depot yard, were relaid. The catch points at the top of the depot ramp had to be held open for departing cars.

A faulty conduit point tongue broke ploughs on three successive trams outside New Cross depot on 29 April 1950, causing a 30min delay; there was another 30min delay there due to a derailment on 15 March 1951.

Delay in crew-changing caused long delays on the westbound track east of the junction. Relief crews sat on garden walls near Pepys Road, while a regulator tried to sort out the mess.

From New Cross one could reach the Embankment by five routes: 35 via Walworth Road; 36 and 38 via the Old Kent Road, and Blackfriars and Westminster respectively; and 40 and 72 via the Oval.

The Malpas Road and Shardeloes Road One-Way System

Trams to Brockley and Forest Hill turned along Lewisham Way, climbing for one-third of a mile to the junction of Malpas Road. Those for Brockley used Malpas Road, returning to New Cross via Shardeloes Road, where the sharp exit curve into Lewisham Way was on a down-gradient.

On 8 February 1948 a tram left the rails in Shardeloes Road, careered 40yd along the pavement and hit a wall. Three people were injured when a route 74 tram ran into a stationary tram in Shardeloes Road at Vulcan Road on 3 November 1951.

The uniting tracks were joined by a trailing crossover at Brockley Cross, where the section feeder box was in the middle of the road. A quiet spot in tram days, now it is busy even on Sundays.

Brockley

A lorry driver was killed on 10 December 1947 when he collided with a route 74 tram in Stondon Park at Honor Oak Park.

A man knocked down by a tram in Brockley Rise on 6 February 1951 died a month later. At the inquest on 10 April, the tram driver stated he was doing 10mph. 'I gonged hard but he never looked. I applied my brakes but he continued across the road.'

The triangular junction at Brockley Rise and that at Rushey Green were the only such junctions where all sides were regularly used after the war.

Forest Hill Terminus

The terminus of routes 35 and 66 in Waldram Park Road was a short double track branch off the main route; it ended in single track. In November 1949 the facing points and crossing at the junction were relaid.

1 March 1952: Queen's Road at Queen's Road station, viewed towards New Cross Gate, with 'E/3' car No 1968. Of the then existing extensive horse-car tracks, alongside the railway on the extreme left, there is now no trace.

14 March 1990: T808 on route 171 replacing the 35 tram route. In the intervening years the bridge girders have been replaced and the abutments altered.

Replacing Bus Services

Route 66 did not run on Sunday; it was based on Camberwell depot until June 1949, then transferred to New Cross until closure. It was the only route to close without any of its track being abandoned: but in April 1991 replacing bus route 36A, Monday-Friday peak hours only, from Victoria to Brockley Rise, ceased.

The southern part of tram route 35 is replaced by bus route 171, Forest Hill-Aldwych, extended Monday-Friday to Islington Green; it deviates from the tram route between County Hall and Aldwych.

All-night tram route 7, New Cross Gate-Savoy Street via Walworth Road and Blackfriars, is covered by bus route N72 and other night routes. Between Camberwell Green and Shooter's Hill, the N72 route mostly follows the course of the 72 tram route.

Left and below:
23 March 1952: Brockley Cross, viewed north towards New Cross, with 'E/3' car No 1962 leaving Malpas Road.

31 January 1988: T1087 on route 171, replacing the 35 tram route, is in Shardeloes Road, used in both directions by buses. Malpas Road is not used today by buses.

15

Lewisham and Grove Park

The Old Kent Road

At the north end of the Old Kent Road, one-third of a mile north of the railway bridge, were New Cross Stadium and Millwall football ground: sometimes special cars were run for supporters. In the Old Kent Road on 3 November 1951 a route 74 tram collided with a bus on route 53A, both carrying spectators to the Millwall ground. The tram derailed near Dunton Road and caused a 20min power failure.

There was a 40min delay on 15 December 1951 when a New Cross-bound tram left the track in the Old Kent Road.

North of the Surrey Canal bridge in the Old Kent Road, disused track could be seen in Bowles Road, on the west side, leading to an old depot. At Canal bridge in those days there were still timber wharves, but the west end of the canal was little used, and there was agitation for it to be filled in. The Surrey Canal closed in 1971 and is now drained, but the bridge still exists. The Livesey Institute and Astoria Cinema on the east side beyond the bridge have gone.

A route 38 car derailed on a curve in New Cross Road early on 27 September 1947. On 5 April 1948 an Embankment-bound 36 was derailed by a broken rail in New Cross Road.

Lewisham Way and the Descent to Lewisham

In Lewisham Way beyond Shardeloes Road were good houses and fine trees. The steep descent of Loampit Hill started at Tyrwhitt Road and continued almost to Lewisham. The River Ravensbourne, then still liable to flooding, was crossed in Loampit Vale.

A crane under tow broke loose on Tanner's Hill on 29 October 1946. It ran down the hill into Lewisham Way, damaging a bus and delaying trams for 20min.

Late in the evening of 2 July 1951, 23 people were injured when a route 54 tram ran into the rear of a tram on route 66, which in turn struck one on route 74. The 66 had been standing at the Malpas Road traffic lights, when the 54 got out of control on the incline. Driver William Nudds of the 74 said later: 'I was flung on my back, and my tram went careering on for 100yd from the force of the collision, yet my brakes had been full on'. The pointsman at Malpas Road added: 'I jumped for my life when I saw the runaway. I thought it would jump the rails and fall on

me'. In respect of the number of injured, it was one of the worst postwar accidents.

In April 1950, parts of both tracks in Loampit Vale were relaid, and the southbound between the Obelisk and Clock Tower received new rails.

Lewisham Obelisk

At Lewisham obelisk, then situated at the Loampit Vale/Lewisham Road junction, was a southbound loading island. Here route 58 diverged to the north. The obelisk, dated 1860, is now at the junction of Lewisham Road and Lewisham Hill.

The busy shopping area between the obelisk and clock tower was served by five tram routes, one to the Embankment, and two each to the City and Victoria. Route 62 cars reversed north of the clock tower on Saturday afternoons.

Below and bottom:
26 August 1951: Stanstead Road at St German's Road, viewed towards Catford, with 'HR/2' car No 128; the stop sign on the left is of London County Council trefoil pattern. The line eastwards from the Stanstead Road/ Brockley Rise junction formed a second route to Rushey Green.

9 May 1987: T874 on route 185 replacing the 58 tram route. This is now a busy part of the South Circular Road.

Above and right:

9 December 1951: Downham Way, at just over one mile long, was the shortest section of overhead on the postwar system. It is seen at Glenbow Road, looking towards Grove Park, with ex-Croydon car No 379, one of the three of the type that were rebuilt. The stop sign is of LCC origin.

4 October 1986: RM1172 on route 36B heads for Grove Park.

Lewisham Clock Tower

Track at Lewisham clock tower, including the facing points, was renewed in September/November 1949. Here routes 46 and 72 diverged along Lee High Road. The road to Rushey Green was wide, with heavy traffic. On the west side south of the clock tower was the site of the 1944 Woolworth flying bomb disaster, then still vacant lots; the new Woolworth has since been closed. Former Tower House, overlooking the clock tower, has fine upper storey reliefs with transport motifs. On the east side of Rushey Green, north of the junction, the Lewisham Hippodrome was replaced by an office block in 1960.

The Sub-Station Explosion at Lewisham

Two men working at a Lewisham High Street sub-station switchroom were electrocuted on 14 February 1946 in an explosion followed by fire. Trams on routes 46, 54, 58 and 72 were halted; buses ran a shuttle service. Breakdown tenders pushed trams from busy crossings, but many were still stranded after two hours.

Brockley Rise-Rushey Green

The curve from Stanstead Road into Catford Hill had a marked superelevation. Trams passed under the railway at Catford station, and over it at Catford Bridge. Parts of both tracks between Catford station and Rushey Green were relaid in September 1950.

Outside the Town Hall at Rushey Green was a triangular junction; at least one tram stop was located on the island in the middle. In March 1949, the southbound track north of the junction was being relaid; in November the trailing points on the west side were renewed.

Downham Way and Grove Park Terminus

The change-pit in Downham Way just east of Bromley Road was the most distant from a London terminus, being just over nine miles from Victoria. Beyond Glenbow Road, Downham Way described an S-curve for its whole length.

Five passengers and both crews were injured when two late trams collided in Downham Way on 5 April 1947. One tram descending the hill crashed into another stationary car.

At 6.50am on 10 June 1948 a route 74 car derailed and broke the overhead in Downham Way, cutting off current on both tracks. A breakdown tender added to the confusion by fouling downed wires.

A route 52 tram ran down the gradient of Downham Way on 5 November 1949, colliding with the rear of a tram on route 74 in heavy rain. The front of the first car was almost completely wrecked, and 15 passengers and the driver were injured.

The turnout at Grove Park terminus handled 40 departures an hour in the peak. The area has declined; at Northover, cars are parked on the pavement as well as at the kerb.

Car Types and Record Runs

Latterly all types of car at New Cross depot, including 'E/1', 'E/3', 'HR/2', ex-Croydon and ex-Walthamstow types, were used on routes 52, 54 and 74.

A record run was made on a route 54 car on 9 December 1951: 'E/3' car No 1913 covered the 10½ miles from Victoria to Grove Park in 50min, averaging 12.6mph. A week later 'HR/2' car No 1882 took 51½min for the run, an average of 12.23mph.

Replacement Bus Services

Route 52 no longer has a replacement. Route 54 is covered by bus route 36B. From Mondays to Fridays, the 74 tram route is replaced by bus route 141; it does not run beyond Catford on Saturdays. All-night tram route 5, Savoy Street-Downham, is covered by bus route N85.

The Saturday morning shopping service between Grove Park and Rushey Green has declined from every 3min to every 12min today.

Top and above:
9 November 1951: Grove Park terminus in Downham Way at Grove Park station, with an ex-Walthamstow car and an 'E/1' behind in the terminal stub. Route 54, with a running time of 62min, was one of the fastest in London.

31 January 1988: A 36B bus replacing the 54 tram route.

The Dockland Route to Greenwich

Poor Tram Headlamps Blamed for Fatality

The driver of a tram which killed an 87-year-old man in the New Kent Road said at the Southwark inquest on 6 January 1950: 'Front lights of trams are still fitted with a shield as in wartime, and they don't give much light'. He had told the police: 'When I first saw the old chap, he was stepping on to the track about 6yd in front of me. I applied emergency brakes . . .'

A bus driver said the man appeared to stumble on the setts, and fall in front of the tram. He added: 'Visibility was poor . . . A dark line is left in the middle of the road by the intersection of the arcs of gas lamps'.

The man died two days after the accident. Recording a verdict of accidental death, the jury added a rider that lighting and condition of the track 'could be improved upon'. The foreman stated: 'Our rider on the condition of the tracks is based on our observations on the spot'.

Bricklayer's Arms

Just south of the Bricklayer's Arms, the tracks ran on each side of a large island. The plough of a tram turning into the Old Kent Road here became jammed on 19 October 1948, causing serious delay; when the car was moved, it broke down again in the New Kent Road.

Tower Bridge Road

There was a large island between the tracks at Tanner Street, 200yd before the Tooley Street junction; on the south side of the junction, the tracks passed on each side of two islands, between which there was a crossover.

London Bridge Station Terminus and Tooley Street

The terminus at Duke Street Hill was beside the London Bridge station viaduct. Double track, as at Borough terminus, showed that an extension had once been planned. This area of warehouses and alleyways teemed with the life of the Port on weekdays.

There was single track in Tooley Street at Stainer Street; the crossover at Bermondsey Street beyond was used by short-working cars, which displayed this destination.

Bermondsey and Rotherhithe

In a visit arranged by the Bermondsey Children's Council, 500 local children travelled in five trams to see a rehearsal of *The Snow Queen* at the Old Vic, Waterloo Road, on 20 December 1948.

There was single track before the long curve into Jamaica Road, at Abbey Street. Approaching Rotherhithe Tunnel, there were two single track sections only 440yd apart, at Marigold Street and at Paradise Street. A sharp right-hand curve took the trams into Lower Road. The east end of Jamaica Road is mainly dual carriageway today.

Trams were delayed for 30min late on 23 February 1948 when a defective plough in Jamaica Road caused power failure.

Surrey Docks

The route passed close to Canada and

Left and below:

24 June 1951: An 'E/1' car about to enter the single track section in Evelyn Street at the Deptford Wharf branch railway bridge in a view looking towards Greenwich.

26 September 1987: A bus on route 1. The bridge abutments and the narrowing in the road remain. The railway has, however, long gone along with many of the buildings on the north side of the road.

Greenland Docks, giving glimpses of shipping not possible from the street. Surrey Docks was extended after great damage in the war, to cover 460 acres. All are now closed, and most filled in.

Most of the peak hour traffic came from the Surrey and other docks. By 1951, the last year of the local trams, the population of Bermondsey had fallen to 61,000, less than half the 1901 figure, due to the war and decline of the docks.

Route 68 Trams Fired On

In February 1949, police were seeking a marksman who apparently disliked trams. On the 7th, three upper deck windows were bro-ken on two route 68 trams within an hour by air-gun pellets in Evelyn Street; a passenger was injured by flying glass. On the night of 8th/9th, a shot thought to have come from an upper floor flat at Dockhead, Bermondsey, broke an upper deck window of a Waterloo-bound tram on route 68. Later another route 68 car had a top deck window broken in New Kent Road.

Temporary Bridge at Deptford Creek

The rolling lift bridge at Deptford Creek, a third of a mile from Greenwich church, was replaced by a temporary bridge in 1949. While the old bridge was being demolished and rebuilt, trams used a temporary lift

Below and bottom:
24 June 1951: 'E/1' car No 591 passes Surrey Docks station in Lower Road at Rotherhithe Old Road in a view looking towards Greenwich.

23 September 1988: The rebuilt station, which has now been renamed Surrey Quays.

Left and below left:

24 July 1949: The new temporary Deptford Creek Bridge on the left is used by inward-bound cars, while outward cars still use the old bridge on the right. The foreground track has been excavated to receive the new connecting curve towards Greenwich. The view is seen looking towards Rotherhithe.

25 February 1990: A bus on route 1 approaches. Note the colour light signals and the signal cabin for controlling the raising of the bridge.

bridge south of the present structure. Centrally-laid tracks occupied most of the roadway, which was about 24ft wide.

This first conduit construction of note since the war was carried out without service interruption. By 17 July westbound cars were using the new bridge; eastbound cars still used the old, and the new eastbound was awaiting connection at both ends.

The new rolling lift bridge was opened in March 1954. Occasionally it is raised to give access to ballast wharves on the south side. North thereof, coasters sometimes lie at the wharf to load scrap metal.

Greenwich Terminus

Routes 68 and 70 terminated in Greenwich Church Street, just north of St Alfege's church. Only the south side of the triangular junction at the church was in regular use. The north-to-west curves served for depot running route 68 and 70 cars to and from New Cross, which supplied all cars for the routes.

Car Types and Replacing Routes

Routes 68 and 70 were latterly worked by '500' series 'E/1s', a few of the oldest 'E/1s', and streamlined 'E/1' car No 1260.

Bus route 47 covers the London Bridge-Deptford part of tram route 70, and bus route 1 Surrey Docks-Greenwich. The route of the 68 tram is served by bus route 188.

17

Lewisham to Woolwich via Eltham

Lewisham-Eltham

The eight miles of route east of Lee Green and Woolwich change-pits formed the largest overhead wire network after the war. Trams changed to overhead at Lee Road, Lee Green, but the change-pit was 200yd beyond at Leyland Road. Just before Eltham Green, at Middle Park Avenue, was the crossover where route 44 cars reversed.

Well Hall Circus

The roundabout at Well Hall Circus was similar to that at Eltham Green, and also had automatic points which did not always function. Since at busy times nearly three times as many cars went via Eltham as via Westhorne Avenue, drivers of trams on route 72 often had to alter points at both roundabouts.

At Eltham Green there was no connection on the west side, and at Well Hall none on the north; route 44 cars could thus not reverse on the Eltham Green roundabout. The sharp curves and extra points were no aid to operation.

Shooter's Hill and Well Hall Common

Beyond Well Hall Circus, the trams climbed to the top of Shooter's Hill; the long ascent suffered from a voltage drop, evidenced by slow running and dimming of tram lights.

An Army lorry leaving the Royal Military Academy on 31 October 1946 was caught between two trams going opposite ways. The tram drivers, two passengers, and the driver of the badly damaged lorry were injured.

Serious Accident on the Descent to Woolwich

Approaching Woolwich, the northbound track followed Grand Depot Road, and the southbound Woolwich New Road, for 440yd; the latter, partially at a lower level, had a steeper gradient.

The trams passed the impressive Royal Artillery Barracks. After uniting briefly, the tracks separated again, the northbound along Green's End, and the southbound along Woolwich New Road.

Four passengers were injured on 18 April 1946 when a route 72 car nearing Beresford Square got out of control descending Grand Depot Road. The tram, half filled with early workers, derailed at a curve, mounted the pavement in Woolwich New Road, and hit three shops.

The Track Layout at Beresford Square Terminus

Routes 44, 46 and 72 terminated in a clockwise loop in Beresford Square, just short of the tracks used by routes 36, 38 and 40. The loading point was at the north end of narrow Woolwich New Road.

There were three connections from the turning circle on to the line to Abbey Wood. The first diverged at the bottom of Green's End and was used by early morning cars

Below and below right:
28 June 1952: Westhorne Avenue, wide and straight, climbs continually towards Well Hall Circus. 'E/3' car No 1939 enters Westhorne Avenue at Eltham Circus.

11 January 1989: L76 on route 122 replacing the 72 tram route between Woolwich and Lewisham.

28 June 1952: One week before closure of the system, 'E/3' car No 1920 passes the south side of Eltham Circus at Westhorne Avenue, viewed towards Eltham church. Trams followed the gyratory traffic system at Eltham Circus, where the automatic points were temperamental. The track on the south side was renewed in June 1951.

14 November 1987: A bus on route 122 replacing the 72 tram route between Woolwich and Lewisham.

Above and right:
September 1951: Plumstead Road, viewed from Beresford Square at Woolwich New Road towards Abbey Wood, with ex-East Ham car No 94. On the left is the high wall of the Royal Arsenal.

15 August 1987: View from a nearer standpoint showing subsequent road widening.

Left and below left:
22 June 1952: Woolwich New Road at Plumstead Road, looking north. The connecting curve from Plumstead Road interlaced with the Beresford Square turning circle. Beyond are the Royal Arsenal buildings.

15 August 1987: L29 on route 178 waits at the zebra crossing. Although The Ordnance Arms on the left remains a Taylor Walker house, the Chef & Brewer house across the road has been demolished.

from Eltham to Greenwich church; there was no return working.

The second connection made a facing junction with line to Greenwich, leaving the turning circle at a large shelter. The third also made a facing connection with the Greenwich line, crossed the turning circle, interlaced with it and joined it at the end of Woolwich New Road. The last two connections were used by cars running to and from Abbey Wood depot, which used a trailing crossover in Plumstead Road: passengers were allowed to join cars on routes 44 and 46 entering service at Abbey Wood

Subsequent road widening at Beresford Square has stranded the old Royal Arsenal entrance in the middle of the road. In World War 1, 75,000 worked at the Arsenal; rapid decline after 1945 led to closure in 1967.

Depot Allocation and Services

Route 44 cars, based at Abbey Wood depot, were of ex-East Ham or ex-West Ham types. Working of route 46 was shared between Abbey Wood and New Cross. All route 72 cars came from New Cross. Latterly, route 46 cars could be of any New Cross type, as well as the occasional East London car: it was one of the most interesting routes for rolling stock.

The eight to 10min headway of route 72 was among the longest on the system; it tended to be slow, and on Sunday ran only from Woolwich to New Cross Gate. Route 44 ran weekdays only.

Replacing Bus Services

Bus route 21 covers tram route 46 between Eltham Church and St George's church. There is no replacement for the 44, and no day route turning from Well Hall Road into Eltham Hill, as did tram routes 44 and 46. Bus route 122 follows the course of the 72 tram route between Woolwich and Lewisham clock tower.

18

New Cross-Abbey Wood

Deptford Wharf Permanent Way Yard

The yard was on the north side of the road, east of Deptford Bridge; exit tracks trailed on to both main road lines. Rail was handled for Rye Lane and Manor House Permanent Way Yards, which had no track connections. Sand used in tramcar sanding gear was sent to depots in works cars.

The Connection from Lewisham to Greenwich

In little more than a mile, between Lewisham obelisk and Greenwich Town Hall, were six single track sections: one of the loops was at the Blackheath Road crossing. Beyond the summit just north of Morden Hill, a down-gradient crossed the old Greenwich Park branch line formation by a moribund bridge. An embankment of this railway may still be seen east of St John's station. Fine old houses still grace Greenwich South Street at Ashburnham Grove, birthplace of Edgar Wallace.

Trafalgar Road and the Tramway Power Station

The former London County Council Tramways power station could be glimpsed from Trafalgar Road, half a mile east of Greenwich church. The still-extant building has a massive arched façade in Old Woolwich Road between Greenwich Park Street and Hoskins Street. At each end of the frontage are sett-paved yards with grooved rail. The south end of the west wall is badly cracked, and '1908' is cast in the rainwater guttering.

The complex, modernised to burn oil in 1972, now supplies power to the Underground. The disused coaling jetty on the Thames is supported on 16 massive piers.

The Blackwall Tunnel Branch

At the end of Blackwall Lane, route 58 tracks passed on each side of a central island. Blackwall Lane and Tunnel Avenue were then thriving industrial areas. Near the terminus were factories and yards. The area was dominated on the east side by East Greenwich Gasworks: the 300ft-diameter gasholder of 1892 was the world's largest. One gasholder was demolished in the early 1980s.

The route 58 terminus was in the middle of the road close to the ornamental portico of the old tunnel of 1897, which had a 24ft-diameter and 16ft-roadway. A quiet spot on Sundays, the café where cyclists rested before braving the sett-paved passage of the Tunnel has gone, together with other old buildings. Today, the Blackwall area is most uninviting.

Charlton Repair Works

The main route beyond Blackwall Lane passed under the Angerstein Wharf branch railway; just west thereof is now a flyover leading to Blackwall Tunnel. The branch line, still in use, no longer reaches the Thames.

Charlton Repair Works was east of the railway bridge, on the north side of the road; a facing connection ran from the eastbound into the present Felltram Way, where often staff cars stood. After the war, ex-West Ham cars performed this duty, but were latterly replaced by two ex-Walthamstow cars after all of that type had been withdrawn.

Below and bottom:
12 August 1951: Lewisham Road, viewed towards Greenwich from the former Albion Road, with 'HR/2' car No 1876.

4 May 1987: View taken from opposite Morden Road School, showing a route 180 bus. The right-hand side has been regraded and little now remains of the property from 40 years ago.

The substantially unaltered buildings are today used by a haulage firm. Large areas are still sett-paved, so that the site of the entrance tracks can still be inferred. Much tram rail and some conduit track exists in the yard. Also to be seen are the sites of two turntables, one of 20ft-diameter, and an 18ft-weighbridge bearing the date '1908'. The course of the connection from the Angerstein Wharf branch into the works is still visible.

Penhall Road Scrap Yard

Slightly less than one mile east of Charlton Works, on the north side of the road, was Penhall Road Yard, where most London trams were scrapped after the war. The entrance track trailed on to the Woolwich Road eastbound. Inside the entrance was a change-pit.

The present Penhall Road marks the eastern boundary of the yard. Between sheds on the west side of this road are still remains of parallel tracks that led on to the traverser. The Penhall Road site is today occupied by two filling stations, a transport firm and a car auction firm, the last of these occupying the area where the trams were scrapped.

Accidents in Woolwich Road

A defective tram derailed in Woolwich Road on 6 August 1949, blocking both tracks for 30min.

An Embankment-bound tram on route 36 ran into the rear of a tram on route 40 in Woolwich Road at Charlton Church Lane in the morning peak of 9 May 1950. A passenger was injured and the track was blocked for 30min.

The rear of a tram was smashed in when an army tank transporter collided with it in Woolwich Road, Charlton, on 3 January 1951.

Central Woolwich

Trolleybus routes 696 and 698, to Dartford via Bexleyheath, and to Bexleyheath via Abbey Wood respectively, terminated west of the Free Ferry. The change-pit beyond was the second most distant from Central London, being nine miles from Blackfriars via the Old Kent Road.

On 20 December 1947 a route 40 tram mounted the pavement in High Street, Woolwich, and crashed into a hoarding.

A sharp right-hand curve into Beresford Street was followed by facing and trailing crossovers. The tracks occupied the whole road; Beresford Street has since been widened on the south side.

The Perrott Street terminus of route 40, starting point of the Last Tram on 5 July 1952, was 440yd east of Beresford Square. As far as the hump-backed Plumstead station bridge, the road was moderately wide; between Beresford Square and the station it is now dual carriageway. The wall of the Royal Arsenal at Beresford Square has been set back as much as 50yd.

Plumstead

East of the station, the track occupied most of the road; there were three single track sections in one-third of a mile, between Ancona Road and Barth Road, then a facing crossover at Riverdale Road. In February 1951 new turnouts were laid in Plumstead High Street; parts of both tracks were renewed in June of the same year.

A tram driver was fined 20s with three guineas costs at Woolwich on 23 August 1949 for dangerous driving in Plumstead High Street. He had knocked a boy off his bicycle at a point where the rails were only 2ft 6in from the kerb.

Wickham Lane to Abbey Wood

Just beyond Wickham Lane there was single track, followed by a loop. The last single track was before the sharp curve into Basildon Road. Part of the eastbound in Bostall Hill was relaid in June 1951. At the bottom of Basildon Road was a lantern-shaped compulsory stop sign. After a right-hand curve into McLeod Road a left-hand curve at the other end brought the line to Knee Hill.

Below and bottom:
29 July 1951: Blackwall Tunnel terminus at Tunnel Avenue, viewed looking north, with 'HR/2' car No 134. Today, the original bore is northbound only, a new tunnel taking southbound traffic.

7 February 1988: The untidy tunnel approach today.

Above and right:

15 June 1952: Woolwich Road at Westcombe Hill (now Farmdale Road), viewed towards Woolwich, with 'E/3' car No 1969. The entrance to Charlton Works was on the left, behind the bridge.

7 February 1988: L128 on route 177 replacing the 36/38 tram routes.

Far right, top and bottom:

22 June 1952: Plumstead High Street at Wickham Lane, viewed towards Woolwich. 'E/1' car No 565 (left) passes ex-East Ham car No 91 on route 46; the latter is on a depot run to Abbey Wood.

13 December 1987: L103 on route 122 turns into Wickham Lane on its way to Bexleyheath.

Abbey Wood Terminus

The Knee Hill terminus, south of Abbey Wood Road, was adjacent to a primitive café typical of the time, and a small shelter, the only tram shelter at a terminus after the war. Cars waiting to enter the terminus stood at the end of McLeod Road.

From Woolwich Ferry to Wickham Lane, trams used the trolleybus positive (right-hand) wire. Beyond Wickham Lane, trams had their own wires, so there were six conductor wires in all.

Abbey Wood Depot

To reach the depot, cars used the facing crossover at the double track terminus, turning left into Abbey Wood Road, where the track was single. First came two facing connections into the shed, then a trailing connection; the single line ended at Crumpsall Street.

Car Types, Services and Fast Runs

Latterly, a large variety of cars was used on routes 36, 38 and 40. Route 40 cars came from New Cross depot. Most of those on routes 36 and 38 were based on New Cross, but some came from Abbey Wood.

The 36/38 route had the best service on the postwar system: the 3min interval between the Elephant and Castle and Abbey Wood was strengthened by extras showing 36X and 38X. Between Woolwich Perrott Street and Blackwall Lane, routes 36, 38 and 40 combined to give less than a 2min interval.

The fastest recorded run on route 36/38 was on 23 April 1950; 'E/1' car No 557 ran the 7¼ miles from the Elephant and Castle to Woolwich Ferry in 37min, averaging 12.57mph. The three miles to New Cross Gate took only 13min.

On 16 February 1952 a '500' series 'E/1' car on route 40 ran the 10 miles from Woolwich Ferry to Charing Cross in 52min, averaging 11.54mph.

Replacing Bus Services

The 177 bus route replaces the 36/38 tram routes east of the Elephant and Castle, but terminates at Plumstead station. Four express journeys each in the morning and evening run between Thamesmead and Victoria, over the former Abbey Wood-Blackfriars 36/38 tram routes.

Journeys over former routes 36, 38 and 40 are arduous due to the infrequent service on the 177 bus route and lack of replacement for the 40 tram route. There is now no through route from Camberwell and Peckham to Greenwich and Woolwich.

Right and below right:
22 June 1952: McLeod Road, corner of Knee Hill, as 'E/3' car No 1945 rounds the curve after leaving Abbey Wood terminus, while 'E/3' No 176 in the foreground waits to enter it.

21 September 1986: Today, the wild sweep of Bostall Heath is now a roundabout.

Far right, top and bottom:
22 April 1951: Abbey Wood Road at Crumpsall Street, viewed east from Abbey Wood depot. The single tongue points were possibly the only set in regular use after the war. On the right is a tower wagon for working on tram and trolleybus overhead.

21 November 1987: Part of the closed bus garage.

PART THREE

19

Preparations for Tramway Abandonment

No More Trolleybuses

Trolleybuses replaced nearly all London trams until withdrawal temporarily ceased in 1940. Despite powers to operate trolleybuses in place of the remaining tramways, it was decided after the war not to extend the trolleybus system.

London Transport stated that trams were to give way to buses, to secure integration with other transport services. This aim has generally been achieved; indeed, many tram replacement bus routes have since ceased.

The Attitude of the Press

London national and evening papers were hostile to trams, which received mostly negative mention, most reports dealing with mishaps. It was easy to persuade the public that trams were obsolete.

South London papers, especially the *South London Press*, were more fair-minded. For a time the *SLP* provided a lively forum on the tramway controversy: enthusiasts may have overstated their case, but it was better to do that than keep silent. There was no other discussion of the tramway question.

The Fate of the Trams is Sealed

On the afternoon of 15 November 1946 London Transport announced that trams would be replaced by buses — 'a more modern and attractive form of transport' — to give greater flexibility and better co-ordination.

South London borough councils welcomed the chance to remodel congested, outdated road layouts after the trams were gone, but feared that buses might not be able to move the crowds. Hence the agitation for Underground extensions, none of which was ever built.

The Inception of the London Transport Executive

On Vesting Day, 1 January 1948, London Transport was still subject to the control of the Minister of Transport, the Rt Hon Alfred Barnes MP, under emergency wartime legislation. The change from London Passenger Transport Board was evident in alteration of name on premises, vehicles and publications; tickets referring to the Board continued to be issued. But tramway policy was unchanged.

On 12 January 1948 its new chairman, Lord Latham, averred that the first aim for 1948 was to continue the 'assault on queues'.

Tramway conversion might have to wait for five years, due to bus shortage: in 1947, £1 million had been spent on the trams to keep them in the highest degree of efficiency. He thought London Transport's first duty was to modernise the bus fleet.

The Postwar Shortage of Buses

After the war, London Transport had ordered 4,000 buses, but only 182 had been delivered by the end of 1947, and 1,007 a year later, when 900 old buses were withdrawn.

The bus shortage was caused by the strict allocation of materials. The Labour Government's priority system ensured that most materials were allocated for exports. A serious shortage of building materials, used mainly to repair bomb damage, also meant that depot conversion could not begin.

Conversion of Tramways Expected to Start in 1950

On 4 March 1949 it was announced that tramway conversion, to take three or four years, might start in 1950. Lord Latham stated that the scheme could start when 1,100 buses were available.

The trams were kept going at a heavy and growing cost. The building of the two new garages and conversion of seven tram depots could proceed with Government sanction. The cost of conversion to bus operation would be nearly £10 million.

Transfers of Routes and Cars Between Depots

Space was made free at Wandsworth and Clapham depots on 8 June 1949 to enable work to start on their conversion. Seventeen trams moved from Wandsworth to Clapham, and 51 from Clapham to New Cross and Camberwell. All route 8/20 turns, and one-third of those on route 22/24, went from Clapham to Telford Avenue; all on route 66 from Camberwell to New Cross; all but one or two on route 10 from Telford Avenue to Norwood; all on route 34 from Clapham to Camberwell; and most on route 28 from Wandsworth to Clapham.

'E/1s' of '1200', '1500', and '1600' series went from Clapham to New Cross for route 66; at first some went to Camberwell, but were exchanged for New Cross cars.

Top and above:

14 August 1949: Blackfriars, Unilever House; 'E/3' car No 161 is about to cross Blackfriars Bridge shortly after the working of route 34 was transferred from Clapham to Camberwell. Until June 1949, 'E/3s' were seen only on routes 12, 16, 18, 26, 28, 31, 33, 35, 42, 48 and 78.

4 October 1986: The Blackfriars Underpass occupies this area today.

'E/1s' of '500' and '1300' series, and streamlined 'E/1' car No 1103 went from New Cross to Camberwell for route 34, which became for a brief spell the most interesting route, seeing a great variety of cars, including 'HR/2s'.

Norwood depot took 'E/3' cars Nos 1913-1918 from Thornton Heath, to help work route 10, which lost its 'Felthams'. Route 22/24 gained 'E/3s'; and from 23 July 1949 'Felthams' were regularly seen. Some '1700' series rebuilt 'E/1s' went from Wandsworth to Clapham for route 26, but never ran on other Clapham routes.

Rebuilt '1300', '1400' and '1500' series 'E/1s', the worst at New Cross, went to Norwood depot for route 10.

On 3 May 1950, as rebuilding spread to Telford Avenue, Clapham resumed nine turns on route 8/20, receiving therefor 'E/1s' in the '1500' series.

Date for the Start of Tramway Abandonment Announced

At the beginning of August 1950, Lord Latham gave October 1950 as the starting date for conversion; work on rebuilding depots had already begun.

A few days later, the newly-formed Tramways Development Association circularised South London MPs, London County Council members, and London Transport and British Transport Commission officials.

The TDC wanted rapid-transit tramways costing £200,000 a mile, with subways for congested areas. Mr S. P. Harris, member of their committee, told the *South London Press*: 'In the outer suburbs, the tramways would . . . surface, and run on lines fenced off from the roadway'.

Closure of Battersea Bridge

Battersea Bridge was closed to all traffic on 17 March 1950, when the collier *John Hopkinson* struck a pier. Route 34 cars had to reverse half a mile short of King's Road, Chelsea, at Parkgate Road, 300yd south of the bridge, and never ran to Chelsea again. At first, destination blinds showed 'LATCHMERE', altered later to 'BATTERSEA BRIDGE'.

At a London County Council meeting on 21 March, the Town Planning Officer said that the vessel owner's liability would be limited to about £10,000, but cost of repair might be higher. On 24 April it was reported that the superstructure had been badly weakened; the bridge would remain closed for several months.

Flatiron colliers, low enough to pass under Thames bridges, were then a familiar sight. On 24 October 1946 the Wandsworth Gas Co's 1,780-ton coasting collier *Mitcham*, the largest ship to navigate above London Bridge, berthed at Wandsworth. It was the first diesel collier on the upper river, 270ft long, with a crew of 19.

Agitation for Underground Extensions

According to a press report of 31 January 1950 Mr Peter Benson, Streatham's Labour candidate, promised to press for an Underground extension from Trinity Road (now Tooting Bec) station to St Leonard's church, Streatham.

The Minister of Transport told Sir Austen Hudson, Conservative MP for North Lewisham, it was reported on 21 April 1950, that the Underground could not be extended from the Oval towards Lewisham within the next two or three years.

The Cost of Removing Tracks and Loss of Rating

Under the British Transport Commission Act of 1948, railways were excluded from valuation lists from 1 April 1948, but tramways and trolleybuses were still subject to rating.

Removal of tracks was expected to be expensive. In May 1950, councils were studying the effects on rates: rating of tracks was a valuable source of income. London Transport paid £45,000 in rates in 1948 — more than £1 million at today's values — for the non-exclusive use of a 16ft-strip of road. Councils were being asked to send a consultant engineer and a legal expert to London Transport to clarify all matters involved in track-lifting.

Under the 1933 London Transport Act, roads need only be reinstated as they had been before tracks were laid down. If the Act were observed, but roads reinstated to modern standards, councils might have to pay the balance. The 19 councils would have to maintain the whole road at great extra cost, when the substitute surface wore out.

Timetable for Tramway Conversion Announced

On 5 July 1950 Lord Latham gave details of the tram-scrapping scheme: trams would go in nine stages between October 1950 and October 1952. Work on depots was going according to plan.

The 830 trams would give way to 1,000 buses; 14 tram routes would be extended under bus operation. Staff recruitment was 'moderately satisfactory'. On the same day it was announced that Leeds had bought 90 'Felthams' at a 'secret figure'.

Training Tram Drivers to Drive Buses

The first batch of tram drivers left Wandsworth depot on the morning of 12 June 1950 to retrain on buses for the first stage of tram replacement. After a four weeks' technical course, they would learn the routes.

Hundreds of drivers, some over 60 with long service, were retrained, and there was a big recruitment drive. Men up to 50 were taken on. Tram drivers were allowed to work up to the age of 70, subject to medicals; these men and others, especially from the permanent way section, were as far as possible transferred to other departments.

A Tramwayman's View of the Conversion

Mr William Botten, 66 years old, retiring after 40 years as electrician at New Cross depot, was reported on 1 September 1950 as saying: '. . . trams are the finest form of transport ever designed. Of course South London could do with a new fleet of trams and better tracks . . .'.

The Laying Out of Penhall Road Yard

Early in January 1950, sleeper tracks were being laid down in Penhall Road Yard at Charlton. The yard was on the north side of Woolwich Road, one mile west of Woolwich Ferry. Penhall Road ran along the eastern boundary. The yard extended 100yd west thereof and some 170yd north from Woolwich Road.

About mid-January the yard was linked with the eastbound track in Woolwich Road. By 12 February a change-pit was being built inside the entrance. Standards and span wires were in place for the overhead by 14 April.

The Penhall Road storage tracks were at right angles to the main road, and connected by a traverser drawing current from the overhead. The yard had an area of 3½ acres, and eventually contained nearly a mile of track laid with old rails.

A London Transport official told the *South London Press*, as reported on 2 May 1950: 'We hope to have a good deal of old tram metal and parts to sell to help towards the cost of conversion'. The yard opened during the summer to receive withdrawals, accident-damaged cars and surplus works cars.

Trams were scrapped in the northeast corner of the yard, just north of the traverser at the north end of the yard. On 26 July 1950,

Below and bottom:
25 September 1950: The final terminus of route 34 at the south end of Battersea Bridge viewed towards Chelsea. Behind 'E/3' car No 167, the abandoned connection to Battersea Wharf Permanent Way Yard branches off to the left.

19 September 1988: Battersea Bridge was in restricted use when this view was taken. Apart from the elderly lamp brackets on the bridge parapets, little remains of the scene 40 years ago. The works of Phillips Mills & Co Ltd, hidden behind the advertising hoardings, have now been replaced by a modern glass office block.

Right and below:

2 July 1950: The newly constructed traverser pit, running west-to-east at the north end of Penhall Road Yard seen looking east towards Penhall Road.

5 October 1988: Today's concreted road transport yard; above the trees the top of two towers can just be identified providing a reference to the earlier photograph. (View taken with permission of Carryfast Ltd.)

rebuilt 'E/1' car No 1322 became the first to be burned. The fire lasted 20min, and was watched by London Transport officials, the fire brigade and local businessmen. It was decided that 1½ trams a day could be disposed of and, occasionally, two trams would be burned on Sundays.

The Camberwell Underground Extension

Camberwell had long tried to get an Underground extension: the impending end of the trams spurred its efforts. Mr G. Dodson-Wells, Public Relations Officer of London Transport addressed the Deptford Arts and Civic Society on 3 November 1948: he could not promise that a Bakerloo Line extension from the Elephant and Castle to Camberwell Green, though badly needed and high on the list of projects, would be completed within five years.

Powers for an extension already existed in 1948. Services over the existing line could be improved by better reversing facilities at Camberwell Green. In 1948 an extension of powers was being sought. Some work had been put in hand, so as to lose no time when authority was received.

It was reported on 17 January 1950 that for some weeks shafts for boring tests were being sunk along the route. It was expected that work would cease after May 1951, in order not to interfere with Camberwell's Jubilee celebrations on the Green.

Southwark Council, then waiting to discuss the siting of the station at Camberwell Gate, was informed in March 1950 that it would not be built: no official reason was given. In 1949 London Transport had hinted that the station had been temporarily shelved, but room would be left for it to be built later.

On 29 September 1950 London Transport announced that the whole scheme had been shelved. During the 20 months of planning, inflation had added £1 million to the cost. The Government had vetoed the project, which would now cost £6 million for 1½ miles of tube.

Below and bottom:
19 September 1950: In Penhall Road Yard on 6 September were works cars Nos 020, 'E/1' No 1383, and rebuilt 'E/1' cars Nos 1385, 1654 and 1762. By the 19th there were eight passenger and three works cars in the yard. From the 27th were added rebuilt 'E/1' cars Nos 1727, 1744 and 1396, the latter having been damaged at Lavender Hill.

5 October 1988: View taken from a nearer standpoint than that above.

20

The Abandonment of the Tramways

The First Tramway Conversion

By 14 February 1950 only 36 trams were left at Wandsworth depot, but after rebuilding it would hold 75 buses. Work had already started on coach shop, tyre store and paint shop. Excavations for the oil pit had filled with 7ft of water: the rear of the shed was only 60yd from the river. The bus garage incorporated east and north walls, some interior buildings and roof trusses.

At 2pm on 30 September 1950 trams started to leave Wandsworth and Clapham for other depots; after service during the evening, trams arrived at Penhall Road every few minutes. The 56 withdrawn cars were 'E/1s' and rebuilt 'E/1s' from New Cross, Camberwell and Norwood depots; four also came from Wandsworth and Clapham. Twenty more 'Felthams' for Leeds went to Penhall Road for storage.

It was raining hard as the last tram on route 34 left Battersea Bridge at 11.55pm on 30 September. Groups stood along the way to Camberwell Green to watch it pass followed by two police cars. At Brixton, two white-jacketed waiters from a café the crew had frequented handed Driver Robert Henna a bottle of whisky. At Camberwell depot an official was heard to say: 'I'm sorry to see them go, we have had plenty of trouble with them — but they've been good old friends'.

The last Stage 1 service car was scheduled to leave Bloomsbury at 12.23am on Sunday 1 October, via Kingsway Subway, to arrive Wandsworth depot at 1.02am. For this last route 31 car there was a wreath from Mrs N. Burgess and her daughter, whose hairdressing saloon was adjacent to York Road.

Routes 12, 26, 28, 31 and 34, and all-night routes 3 and 26, ceased to run. There had also been a morning peak hour turn from London Bridge (Borough) to Wandsworth High Street via the Embankment, designated EX.

Abandoned sections were: Vauxhall-Wandsworth High Street and Clapham Junction; Princes Head-Clapham Junction; Latchmere Hotel-Battersea Bridge; Lambeth Bridge-Marshalsea Road; and Brixton-Loughborough Junction.

Tram routes 12, 26, 28, 31, 34 and all-night route 3 were replaced by bus routes 44, 168, 169, 170, 45 and 288 respectively. The 612 trolleybus route, also based at Wandsworth depot, was covered by the 44 bus route, London Bridge (Borough)-Mitcham, Fair Green. Route 168 was extended to Farringdon Street, and to Wandsworth High Street. Route 170 was diverted at Rosebery Avenue to Well Street, Hackney. Route 45 was extended to Farringdon Street, and later to South Kensington. All-night route 288 was extended to Wandsworth and Farringdon Street.

Route 168 was the first to use the inner Embankment tram track. Bus drivers had to be careful: the space between kerb and oncoming trams was only 10ft, and one or two plane trees had to be sacrificed.

For Stage 1, 129 buses stored at Edgware crossed London at intervals to their garages. The first replacing bus was on route 168 from Wandsworth garage at 3.46am on 1 October, in place of tram route 26. RT 1869 was driven by Mr R. C. Raikes and conducted by Mr R. E. Bishop. At first, buses entered the garage over the traverser.

From 1 October, Clapham received 32 buses for route 45; in January 1951, 97 more were to be based there. To make space for rebuilding, 50 buses were to be parked on a lot in Clapham Park Road, to the anger of local shopkeepers: today, who would care? Conversion of Clapham depot was scheduled for completion in 1952.

Scrapping Trams at Penhall Road

After 37 years' service and running over 1½ million miles, rebuilt 'E/1' car No 1656 was

Far left, top and bottom:
25 September 1950: Lavender Hill from the top of Falcon Road, viewed towards Vauxhall, during the last week of trams in this area. Behind 'E/1' car No 1824 on route 28 are two 'E/3s' on route 34.

27 April 1987: D/DM2557 on route 156 passes the frontage of Arding & Hobbs – a survivor from 40 years earlier – as it makes its way towards Morden.

Above left and left:
15 April 1950: In November 1949 Clapham depot was being rebuilt for bus operation; inspection, docking, and wash pits were being built, and a pit 25ft deep for fuel oil sunk. By 14 February 1950 half the space had been concreted over, and tram inspection pits filled up to within 9in of ground level. This view shows the rear of the depot from the south.

5 November 1988: The rear of the disused bus garage.

Right and below right:
11 November 1950: Tooting Broadway, viewed north from Tooting High Street towards Balham, with Saturday morning peak hour extras. 'E/1' car No 1837 is on route 6 and, in the background, an 'E/3' on route 22 turns into Mitcham Road.

19 December 1986: D/DM2590 on route 57 waits at a red traffic light behind an RM on route 49.

Below and below right:
7 April 1951: Late in the afternoon, rebuilt 'E/1' car No 839 stands at the entrance to Purley depot. This car made a ceremonial last run for the Croydon and Purley Chambers of Commerce later in the day.

29 September 1988: Although still clearly the same building, Purley depot has now been converted into a DIY shop.

burned at Penhall Road on 2 October 1950. Six of the 20 'Felthams' in store had gone by the 21st. George Cohen & Sons (the 600 Group) had scrapped 32 trams by 29 October.

Trams were stripped of fittings, then tipped off the trucks, which were cut up. The body was burned to separate wood from metal. Serviceable equipment was salvaged for further use.

Awaiting scrapping on 31 December were 'Felthams' Nos 2126 and 2164, burned out at Brixton Hill depot in November, and four 'E/1s'.

Conversion of the Clapham Routes

At a Clapham Chamber of Commerce meeting on 12 November 1950, members were told that London Transport had powers to widen the High Street entrance of Clapham depot: displaced traders should be compensated. The Chamber agreed to renew objections to the bus garage: the High Street entrance for trams was about 12ft wide, but the garage as completed had an extensive forecourt, entailing demolition of shops.

The depot occupied a large central site in Clapham, at street level mostly fronted by small shops in High Street and Clapham Park Road, with inconspicuous entrance and exit. The demolition of shops at this time played a part in Clapham's postwar decline.

The last tram from Tooting Broadway, a route 10 car bound for Norwood depot, left at 12.21am on 7 January 1951, crewed by Driver Miles and Conductor Frost.

At 12.16am a special tram with members of the Balham & District Chamber of Com-

Above and right:
26 July 1951: 'HR/2' car
No 1870 about to enter
Newington Butts from
Walworth Road, at the
Elephant and Castle
Northern Line station.

29 October 1988: The
Northern Line station today.

merce had left Tooting Broadway: tickets cost 5s each. It was escorted by army dispatch riders to the Odeon, Balham Hill, which remained open until midnight for celebrations. When the last service tram entered Clapham depot that night, it had been stripped of many fittings.

Sections closed in Stage 2 were: County Hall-Vauxhall; Oval-Wimbledon; and Tooting Broadway-St Leonard's church, Streatham.

Routes 2, 4 and 10 became bus routes 155W, 155B and 95 respectively; 95 was extended to Cannon Street. Route 6 was replaced by bus route 189, extended to Cannon Street, but diverted at Clapham Common to replace bus routes 5 and 5A. Routes 22 and 24 became 50 and 104: Horse Guards Avenue-Telford Avenue (via Brixton), and to Tooting, The Mitre (via Clapham). Buses 57 and 57A replaced tram routes 8 and 20: Victoria to Tooting Broadway (via Brixton), and to St Leonard's church (via Clapham). All-night tram route 1 became bus route 287: Southcroft Road daytime circular services ceased and peak hour service was reduced.

Opposition to Retention of the Tramway Telephone System

A special meeting of Battersea Borough Council was called on 29 December 1950 to oppose parts of the British Transport Commission's 1950 Bill, under which the BTC was to retain use of the tramways telephone system. It would confer powers to break up any street where equipment was laid, and to interfere with sewers and drains. The Council accepted a recommendation that a petition be presented to either or both Houses of Parliament.

Croydon Loses its Trams

At midnight on 1 January 1950 all trams at Thornton Heath depot moved to Purley, previously a store, but also used for repainting trams. By 26 February the whole Thornton Heath complex had gone to make way for a bus garage.

During conversion of Telford Avenue depot, Brixton Hill depot was reopened as an annexe. One report claims that work on Telford Avenue started on 18 December 1949: the smaller southern shed was demolished first. The new bus garage was to cover the entire site: the water main which passed between the tram sheds was relaid in a subway. The reservoir east of the garage still exists.

By 14 February 1950 the southern shed was reduced to one wall and a mass of girders; only 12 of the 34 cars once there were left, without light at night, or current by day. Demolition and levelling employed 42 men. On 7 April four works cars were in the shed; the two southernmost roads, on a ramp, were still used for service trams.

Work on the northern Telford Avenue shed started about the end of 1950. The only parts retained were the end walls. The new garage was for 107 buses, against 90-100 trams.

'Felthams' withdrawn for storing at Penhall Road had been replaced at Telford Avenue by 'E/3' cars from Wandsworth and Camberwell. By the end of 1950, about 30 'E/3s' were running from Telford Avenue, but fewer were needed after 6 January 1951, to work routes 16 and 18 only.

Brixton Hill was empty by the early afternoon of 7 April 1951. Among trams run into Penhall Road that day were 40 'Felthams', car No 1, and 'ME/3' car No 1444, the last remaining cars of modern appearance. Although finally withdrawn on 7 April, the last of the 90 'Felthams' did not leave Penhall Road for Leeds until October. The stock at Purley and Telford Avenue depots, including ex-Croydon and ex-Walthamstow cars, was moved to New Cross.

Tramways abandoned at Stage 3 were: Lambeth Town Hall, Brixton-Purley; the Thornton Heath branch; and Elephant and Castle-The Horns, Kennington. It was the only stage to involve more overhead than conduit.

On 8 April 1951 tram routes 16 and 18 became bus route 109, via Westminster or via Blackfriars. The 190 bus route in place of the 42 tram route was extended from Coombe Road to the Swan and Sugar Loaf.

Replacement of Tramway Stop Signs

Tram stop signs were replaced by temporary signs at least a week before conversion. Stops at road junctions were set back to improve traffic flow, but interchange was less convenient. Stops for opposite directions for the buses were further apart than with the trams.

Bus stop signs were of the then-new aerofoil design, on a concrete post, with route information facing the pavement. Similar signs and posts were still being erected in 1991. Each early tramway conversion required the erection of some 100 new bus stop signs, hooded until the buses commenced.

Last Trams in Bermondsey and Rotherhithe

'E/1' car No 587, chartered by the Electric Traction Group, made the last journey from Tooley Street at 11.35pm on 10 July 1951 draped in black cloth.

The last service car arrived at New Cross depot via Greenwich shortly after midnight on 11 July. The driver, 62-year-old Mr James Jameson, had driven trams on routes 68 and 70 for 38 years; the next day he took out a bus.

'E/1' car No 1260, with streamlined top deck, and latterly seen on route 68, appears to have been withdrawn at this time. This Stage 4 of the conversion occurred on a

Tuesday, but all others took place on a Saturday. Thirty-three trams were displaced; route 72 was cut back from London Bridge (Borough) to its previous Savoy Street terminus on the Embankment.

Sections abandoned were: London Bridge station-Greenwich Church; Waterloo station-St George's Circus; Blackfriars Road-London Bridge (Borough); and Bricklayer's Arms-Tower Bridge. Stages 4 and 5 were the only ones not to involve overhead mileage.

Tram routes 68 and 70 were replaced by bus routes 188 and 70. Route 188 was extended from Waterloo to Chalk Farm, and route 70 from Tooley Street to Waterloo. The first route 188 bus left Peckham Bull Yard garage for Greenwich church at 4.34am on 11 July.

Closure of the Dog Kennel Hill Routes

Rebuilding of Camberwell depot had started on 5 March 1951. The two sheds were reconstructed as one bus garage.

A large crowd saw the last service car enter Camberwell depot on 6 October 1951. A few hours later, the first replacing bus was taken out by 68-year-old Mr Alfred Lee, a tram driver for 42 years: the 50-year age limit for bus drivers was indeed somewhat elastic!

A last day tour of the Dulwich routes was organised by Mr P. Davies. The special, driven by Mr Alfred Sharman, followed the last service car into Camberwell depot.

On 6 October routes 56, 58, 60, 62, 66, 84 and all-night route 7 ceased. Sections abandoned were: Camberwell Green-Forest Hill; the Peckham Rye branch; Lewisham obelisk-Greenwich Town Hall; and Woolwich Road-Blackwall Tunnel.

Tram routes 56 and 84 were replaced by bus route 184, extended from Peckham Rye to Brockley. Routes 58, 60, 62, 66 and all-night route 7 were replaced by bus routes 185, 176A, 176, 36A and 286. At Victoria, buses turned in the width of Vauxhall Bridge Road, short of the tram terminus.

The '1800' series 'E/1s' were transferred to New Cross depot, which received some '100' series 'HR/2s' for route 35, the longest postwar route, and now the last with all-conduit operation. The rest of the '100' series 'HR/2s' were scrapped, as the type had no trolley poles. Until then, only 'E/1' cars had been scrapped.

Last Trams to Victoria and Grove Park

Stage 6 of the abandonment took place on 5 January 1952 when routes 48, 52, 54, 74, 78 and all-night route 5 ceased. The last standard 'E/1s', the ex-Walthamstow, and the ex-Croydon cars were withdrawn, but the '500' series 'E/1s' still remained. Two ex-Walthamstow cars still existed on 15 February for staff duties.

The tram routes were replaced by bus routes 48, 149, 69, 179, 178 and all-night route 285 respectively. Sections closed were: Victoria-Brixton; Camberwell Green-Herne Hill; St George's church-Elephant and Castle; Lewisham clock tower-Grove Park; and Rushey Green-Stanstead Road/Brockley Rise.

Removal of Tram Tracks

Wandsworth, the first council faced with the problem of disused tram tracks, was to be asked on 23 January 1951 to approve a three-year scheme for lifting 11½ miles of tracks, and road resurfacing and widening. The Council expected to recover £193,000 of the £428,000 bill from London Transport. Work was not expected to begin until early 1952, because of the planning involved, and police restrictions during the Festival of Britain. Track-lifting would yield about 6,000 tons of steel: tenders were to be invited at once. Due to tramway abandonment, Wandsworth had given roads carrying tramways minimum attention since 1937.

Mr George Strauss, Minister of Supply, announced in the Commons at the end of April 1951 that steel production might have to be reduced, due to a shortage of iron-ore and scrap. Arrangements were being made between industry and local authorities for financial help to lift tram rails. When Mr C. W. Gibson (MP for Clapham) pointed out that miles of track were being covered up, Mr Strauss promised to investigate.

Later Mr Strauss wrote to Mr Gibson that he was pursuing the matter with the Ministry of Transport: 'I understand that . . . road reconstruction following the scrapping of the London tramway system . . . would make available about 30,000 tons of rails . . . as scrap. The steel industry would if necessary make special contributions . . . to facilitate the recovery of rails'. Thus the steel industry had a stake in tram-scrapping: much track at points and crossings was of manganese steel. It is sad that much valuable, newly-laid track should have been valued only as scrap.

It was announced on 18 May 1951 that the Ministry of Transport had vetoed track-lifting and road works in Wandsworth under defence regulations limiting capital expenditure.

In February 1952 the Lewisham Borough Engineer stated after experiments in London Road, Forest Hill, that removal of one yard of double track and road reinstatement cost £10. The Council was to be asked on the 27th to spend £10,000 on lifting the rest of the track in the road. It was estimated that payment from London Transport and sale of scrap steel would cover the £188,000 that Lewisham was allowed to spend on track-lifting.

Closure of the Kingsway Subway

It was reported on 9 June 1950 that a census was to be taken of southbound traffic about

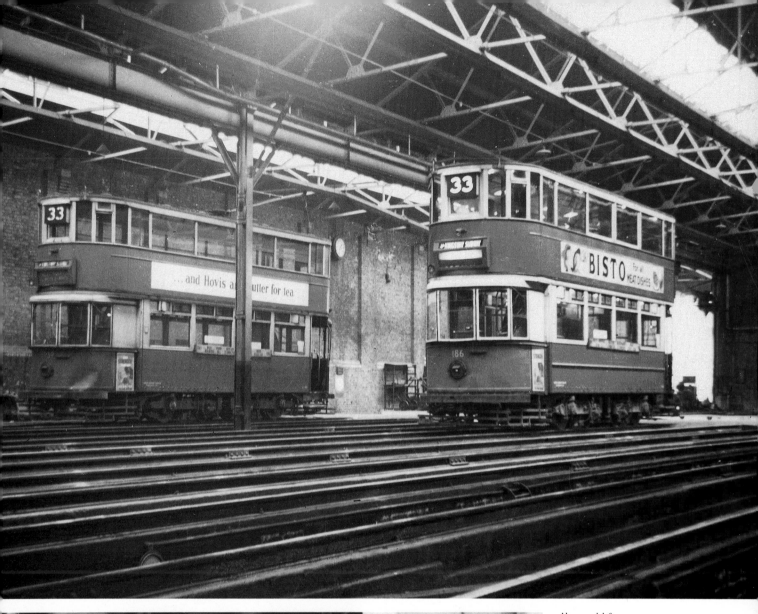

Above and left:
5 April 1952: The interior of Norwood depot on the afternoon of the last day of operation, with 'E/3' cars Nos 1939 and 186. The entrance is on the right.

4 August 1987: In this view the entrance appears in the centre background. (View taken with permission of Howard Smith Papers.)

Above and right:

28 June 1952: Ex-East Ham car No 93 turns from Well Hall Road into Eltham High Street during the last week of the tramways. The last week, 29 June to 5 July, was styled 'Last Tram Week'. All cars, except the ex-West Ham type, carried upper deck posters. Souvenir tickets were issued: on 5 July up to 2s 6d was asked for them unofficially.

23 August 1987: A bus on route 161 passes the former Burton's shop which now serves as a fast food restaurant.

Above and left:

1 July 1952: The entrance to New Cross depot from New Cross Road four days before the system closed. Ex-East Ham car No 86 is in the foreground; behind it, an 'E/3' stands between the levers of the catch points.

31 January 1988: An empty-running route 89 bus leaves the now rebuilt New Cross garage.

the 14th/15th, in Southampton Row near the Kingsway Subway entrance. No decision had been taken on the use of the Subway; only 20ft wide, with sharp bends and buttresses, it was unsuitable for motor traffic. Lord Latham stated on 5 July that future use of the Subway was being discussed.

At about 12.07am on Sunday 6 April 1952 the last southbound service car via the Subway, a tram on route 35 from Bloomsbury to Camberwell Green, left the southern portal at Waterloo Bridge.

A few minutes later, the last service car to use the Subway, a northbound tram on route 35 from Westminster to Highgate, entered the southern portal: the gates were closed behind it. It had left Westminster at 12.02am, and climbed the Bloomsbury ramp at 12.10am, crewed by Driver Keir and Conductor Howes. On its dash was a wreath with a note: 'Farewell, from one faithful friend to another'. As the car left the northern exit, the Subway was officially closed.

These most emotional scenes of the abandonment made a great impression. The closure of this rapid-transit link has remained an embarrassment from that day to this.

The pointsman who sent the last tram into the Subway, 71-year-old Mr Lamb, had done this duty for the previous four years, after 40 years of driving: he was to be found a new job!

As the last route 35 car climbed the Bloomsbury ramp, down came a special with the Mayor of Holborn and his councillors, on a last ride from Theobalds Road to Westminster and back.

In the early morning of 6 April, 52 trams went to Penhall Road: 13 from Holloway depot; 21 from New Cross; and 18 from Norwood. Norwood depot was closed, but Holloway still worked trolleybuses.

On 6 April 1952 tram routes 33 and 35 and all-night 35 were replaced by bus routes 171 and 172 and all-night 172. Sections abandoned were: Savoy Street-Manor House; Islington Green-Archway station; St George's Road; Elephant and Castle-Camberwell Green; Kennington Gate-West Norwood; and Lewisham Way-Forest Hill via Brockley.

The Campaign for Modernisation of the Tramways

In an interview with the Brixton Free Press on 10 October 1948 Mr J. W. Fowler, chairman of the Light Railway Transport League, claimed that 90% of the 6,000 persons polled in South London wanted modern trams.

On 10 March 1950 a Tramway Development Council plan to revolutionise travel was revealed. It proposed fenced-off high-speed tramways from the Oval to Purley and to Grove Park, and duplication of the Underground from Kennington to the Oval, enabling Edgware Line trains to link up with the tramways. Eighty-passenger single-deckers

with rubber-insert wheels and air-doors would be coupled in the peak. The new lines would be partly in subway, with stops further apart, halving travelling time.

The LRTL was also campaigning for the trams. At a Streatham public meeting on 25 March 1950 a resolution was passed that scrapping be delayed until a modern tram supplied by the LRTL had been demonstrated in London: London Transport declined the offer. An LRTL pamphlet, *London Needs Modern Trams*, asked: 'Do you think it is worth £10 million to replace present trams by buses relying on imported fuel?'.

Reconstruction of New Cross and Abbey Wood depots

Proposals to convert New Cross depot into a bus garage and provide a second entrance were to be opposed by Deptford Council, it was reported on 31 December 1948. A Parliamentary Bill empowered the British Transport Commission to acquire land compulsorily in Pepys Road for the new entrance and to extend the complex.

Deptford Council stated it would cost at least £7,000 to reconstruct Pepys Road for buses, and thought that the BTC should do the work. Residents of Pepys Road, described as the 'best in the borough', protested to the London County Council and London Transport about the new bus entrance: they were told it would be unobtrusive and that no buses would be parked in the street.

Demolition of New Cross depot was well under way by 5 March 1951. Some cars used Penhall Road as a depot: in the morning, cars running from there could be distinguished by the frost layer on their roofs. Conversion of New Cross was not completed until after the last trams ran: then the largest garage, it accommodated 300 buses.

On 12 December 1950 it was announced that work would soon start on a new garage at Peckham High Street. It was one of two new garages built for the tramway conversion; the other was at Stockwell. At 5am on 2 May 1951 the first bus left Bull Yard, Peckham.

Demolition had been proceeding for some time at Abbey Wood by March 1951. The original rear wall was retained.

The Tramways During the Final Three Months

Routes 36, 38, 40, 44, 46 and 72 survived until the end of operation. All ran daily except 44, which did not run on Sundays. New Cross and Abbey Wood depots were still in use.

The remaining routes were worked by ex-West Ham, ex-East Ham, 'E/3', '1800' series 'HR/2', and '500' series 'E/1' cars, and car No 2 — in all about 160 vehicles.

Enthusiasts' Reaction to Final Abandonment

On 4 July 1952 the LRTL commented: 'Londoners will . . . have to find the total cost of road maintenance . . . Tomorrow we come to . . . the blackest day in London's tramway history'. LRTL member Mr W. Ackerman had large posters placed all over southeast London, listing his acid comments.

The Last Day of the Tramways

On the last day of the tramways, Saturday 5 July 1952, services were poor, since trams were progressively withdrawn into Penhall Road Yard from early afternoon.

Scenes bordering on hysteria occurred as regular travellers waited in vain, squeezed off by joy-riders. Trams were besieged by paper-hatted crowds, forcing drivers to stop, to allow them to board overcrowded trams. Several women fainted in the crush.

Last Tram from the Embankment

Some last cars were unlit, fixtures having been torn away. Police turned a blind eye to those who put pennies on the track to be squashed into souvenirs.

A crowd surrounded the last car from Savoy Street, due to leave at 11.38pm. After the last tram had left Westminster, many grovelled in the roadway to collect tickets which had fallen from it. The last tram south via Blackfriars Bridge crept over unlit at midnight: all bulbs had been taken for souvenirs. Some conductors paid in as much as £20 at the end of the day — the highest amount ever!

The Last Tramcar in Public Service

The last service car was preceded by several full of revellers, stressing the carnival nature of the last day.

When the last service tram, a route 40 car, left Woolwich Perrott Street at 11.57pm, it had difficulty penetrating the crowds. 'E/3' car No 1951 was preceded by two police cars. The driver, Mr Alfred Fuller, had joined the tramways in 1931; Mr William Bedford first conducted in 1914. Mr John Cliff, deputy chairman of London Transport, and Alderman Albert Morris, Mayor of Deptford, took turns driving.

The Reception Committee at New Cross Depot

Waiting for the last tram at New Cross depot was a committee headed by Lord Hurcomb, chairman of the British Transport Commission, and mayors of six southeast London boroughs.

Among official guests was Mr George Harvey, chief operating clerk of Central Road Services. In 1903 he had issued souvenir tickets at the opening of the first London County Council electric line to Tooting.

Inside the depot, speeches were made by Lord Latham and others to the press, standing round a table bearing trams made of sugar: this ludicrous touch summed up the official attitude to trams. The privileged few then formed a group at the white line where the last tram was to be received.

At 1.15am on Sunday 6 July 1952, 45min late, car No 1951 arrived at New Cross depot, to be surrounded by a crowd estimated at over 20,000. Upon entering the depot, No 1951 had to be towed off a dead section by 'E/3' car No 1931.

Outside the depot, the crowd watched stripped shells of trams making their way to Penhall Road Yard: the last did not leave until about 3am.

Stage 8 Replacing Services and Sections Abandoned

Routes 36 and 38 were replaced by the 177 bus route. The 163 bus route took over the 40 tram route, terminating at Horse Guards Avenue. The 46 tram route was replaced by the 182 bus route, extended to Cannon Street. The 186 bus route covered the route of the 72 tram only between Woolwich and Lewisham. The 44 tram route was not replaced.

The lines closed were: the Embankment circle via Westminster and Blackfriars-St George's Circus; St George's Circus-Abbey Wood via Old Kent Road; Christchurch, Lambeth-New Cross Gate via Oval; Southwark Bridge-Bricklayer's Arms; Marquis of Granby-Woolwich, Beresford Square, via Eltham; and Westhorne Avenue.

The system closed three months earlier than planned, due to the combining of Stages 8 and 9. The approximately 27 miles closed was equivalent to half the size of the Sheffield or Edinburgh systems. But Edinburgh took four years to convert 50 miles and Liverpool 10 years for 92 miles: London Transport achieved 60 miles a year.

Epilogue

The tramway conversion had cost about £10 million. About half was for 1,100 replacing buses, the rest for depot conversion. Possibly about £2 million was expended on lifting tracks which would have cost £5 million to lay in 1952 . . .

. . . It had been a fine day at the height of summer, and several days elapsed before the rails rusted. Walking home after saying farewell to the trams, it was hard to believe that one would never see them again.

Bibliography

ABC of London Trams and Trolleybuses, Ian Allan, 1949.
Balham, Tooting & Streatham News and Mercury.
British Transport Commission Reports and Accounts for 1948.
Brixton Free Press.
The Buildings of England: London 2 South, Bridget Cherry & Nikolaus Pevsner, Penguin, 1983.
Buses of London Fleetbook — 1990, London Omnibus Traction Society.
Croydon Times.
Daily Mail.
Evening News.
Evening Standard.
London County Council Survey of London, 1951.
The London Encyclopaedia, edited by Ben Weinreb & Christopher Hibbert, 1983.
London Transport Tramways Handbook, D. W. Willoughby & E. R. Oakley, 1972.
News of the World.
Observer.
South London Observer.
South London Press.
South Western Star.
Star.
Sunday Dispatch.
Sunday Times.

Appendices

Appendix 1

Trams Observed in Service between 1949 and 1952:

'HR2 Exp': 1
'E1r Str': 2
ex-East Ham 'EH': 81-100
'HR2': 101-11/3-22/6-8/32-47/9-59
'E3': 160-204/6-10
ex-West Ham 'WH': 295-302/4-12/31-44
ex-Croydon 'CCT': 375/7-95/7-9
'E1': 552/4-68/70-5/7-82/4-96/8-601, 802/36/9/40, 916/36/40/7/8/53/60/1/78/81/2/4/5/93/4-6, 1003/5/7/9/17/9/22/4/5/30/2/3/8/42/9/83/7-90/2/4/6, 1103/28/37/40/2-5/63/70-2/4/5/7/82/90/91/5, 1204/8/11-3/5/6/8-20/3/5/6/7/30/1/3/44/6-8/50-52/55/60/7/70/5/91, 1310/2/6/7/50/2/3/5/57-9/61-3/5/6/8-70/5/7/8/80-8/90-2/5-7/9, 1400-2/6-10/3-5/9/22/23/78/80/1/5-9/91-6/8/9, 1500-4/7/8/14/20/5/7/9-34/7/8/

40-2/4-9/55/7/61-71/3/4/6/7/9/81/2/7-90/2-9, 1601-4/6/8/10/12-4/7-9/21/4/6-31/6/8/40/2-8/50-64/7/9-76, 1727/30/43/4/58/61-4/6/8-73/5/7-9/81-7/90/1/3-9, 1801-6/9-15/7-20/2-4/6-30/2-41/3-51

'ME3': 1444
'HR2': 1854-64/6-80/2/4/5/7/8/90-7
'E3': 1904-39/41-66/8-71/4/5/7/9-81/4/6-2003
ex-Walthamstow 'K': 2042/3/5-50/2-61
'Feltham'/'UCC': 2066/8-71/3-90/2-8, 2100-8/10-2/4-21/3-9/31-62/4/5
'UCC Exp': 2167

The following were rebuilds: Nos 127, 379/80/98, 836/9, 936/40/7/8/53/60/78/81/2/4/5/94-6, 1003/9/17/22/24/33/42/87-90, 1103/44/77/90/1/5, 1212/5/6/46-8/60/75, 1310/52/3/7/9/65/6/8-70/5/7/80-2/4-8/91/2/6/97, 1400-2/8/22/81/91/2, 1500/2/7/8/14/20/34/8/41/5/7/63/4/6/9/74/6/7/9/87/90/9, 1606/8/10/4/9/36/42/3/5/7/8/50/2/4-6/61/76, 727/30/143/4/58/61-3/46/8-73/5, 1884/5/7/90/3.

Appendix II

Evening Peak Hour Turns on Routes 2 and 4 until 18 October 1949

Duty No	18	19	20	21	22	23	24	25	26	27	28	29	30	1	2
Balham	4.38	4.42	4.46	4.50	4.54	4.58	5.02	5.06	5.10	5.14	5.18	5.22	5.26	5.30	5.34
Clapham Cmn	4.46	4.50	4.54	4.58	5.02	5.06	5.10	5.14	5.18	5.22	5.26	5.30	5.34	5.38	5.42
Stockwell	4.51	4.55	4.59	5.03	5.07	5.11	5.15	5.19	5.23	5.27	5.31	5.35	5.39	5.43	5.47
Oval	4.56	5.00	5.04	5.08	5.12	5.16	5.20	5.24	5.28	5.32	5.36	5.40	5.44	5.48	5.52
Westminster	–	5.10	–	5.18	–	5.26	–	5.34	–	5.42	–	5.50	–	5.58	–
Elephant	5.03	–	5.11	–	5.19	–	5.27	–	5.35	–	5.43	–	5.51	–	5.59
Savoy St	–	5.14	–	5.22	–	5.30	–	5.38	–	5.46	–	5.54	–	6.02	–
Blackfriars	5.13	5.17	5.21	5.25	5.29	5.33	5.37	5.41	5.45	5.49	5.53	5.57	6.01	6.05	6.09
Savoy St	5.16	–	5.24	–	5.32	–	5.40	–	5.48	–	5.56	–	6.04	–	6.12
Elephant	–	5.27	–	5.35	–	5.43	–	5.51	–	5.59	–	6.07	–	6.15	–
Westminster	5.20	–	5.28	–	5.36	–	5.44	–	5.52	–	6.00	–	6.08	–	6.16
Oval	5.30	5.34	5.38	5.42	5.46	5.50	5.54	5.58	6.02	6.06	6.10	6.14	6.18	6.22	6.26
Stockwell	5.35	5.39	5.43	5.47	5.51	5.55	5.59	6.03	6.07	6.11	6.15	6.19	6.23	6.27	6.31
Clapham Cmn	5.40	5.44	5.48	5.52	5.56	6.00	6.04	6.08	6.12	6.16	6.20	6.24	6.28	6.32	6.36
Balham	5.48	5.52	5.56	6.00	6.04	6.08	6.12	6.16	6.20	6.24	6.28	6.36	6.36	6.40	6.44

Route 2: To the Embankment via Westminster Bridge, returning via Blackfriars Bridge.
Route 4: To the Embankment via Blackfriars Bridge, returning via Westminster Bridge.
The above represents a portion of routes 2 and 4 only.

Appendix III

Record Runs on London Tramcars

Date	Car	Route	Distance	Speed	Timings	
23 April 1950	'E/1' 557	Elephant-Woolwich Ferry	7.75	12.57	Elephant	6.04pm
					New Cross Gate	6.17
					Blackwall Lane	6.30
					Woolwich Ferry	6.41
24 December 1950	'E/3' 184	Savoy St-Manor House	5.25	11.89	Savoy St	4.51½pm
					Holborn	4.57
					Angel	5.01½
					Balls Pond Road	5.09½
					Manor House	5.18
14 January 1951	'E/3' 1908	Purley, Royal Oak-Charing Cross	13.00	11.47	Purley, Royal Oak	3.55pm
					West Croydon	4.05½
					St Leonards	4.28½
					Lambeth Town Hall	4.39
					Oval	4.45½
					Elephant	4.51
					Charing Cross	5.03
4 March 1951	'E/3' 202	Purley, Royal Oak-Elephant	10.75	11.22	Purley, Royal Oak	4.47½pm
					West Croydon	4.56½
					Thornton Heath Pond	5.03
					St Leonards	5.18
					Lamberth Town Hall	5.30½
					Oval	5.38½
					Elephant	5.45
11 March 1951	'E/3' 1913	Purley, Terminus-Elephant	11.25	12.27	Purley	4.56pm
					West Croydon	5.07½
					Thornton Heath Pond	5.14
					St Leonards	5.27½
					Lambeth Town Hall	5.38½
					Oval	5.45
					Elephant	5.51
1 April 1951	'Feltham' 2160	Purley, Terminus-Charing Cross	12.50	11.63	Purley	5.23½pm
					West Croydon	5.35
					Thornton Heath Pond	5.42
					St Leonards	5.56
					Lambeth Town Hall	6.07
					Oval	6.15
					Westminster	6.25½
					Charing Cross	6.28
20 May 1951	West Ham 337	Abbey Wood-Elephant	10.50	11.25	Abbey Wood	4.36pm
					Beresford Square	4.49
					Blackwall Lane	5.04
					Greenwich Church	5.09
					New Cross Gate	5.18
					Elephant	5.32
9 December 1951	'E/3' 1913	Victoria-Grove Park	10.50	12.60	Victoria	12.50pm
					Oval	12.57½
					Camberwell Green	1.01½
					New Cross Gate	1.13
					Lewisham	1.22
					Rushey Green	1.29
					Downham	1.34½
					Grove Park	1.40

Date	Car	Route	Distance	Speed	Timings	
16 December 1951	'HR/2' 1882	Victoria-Grove Park	10.50	12.23	Victoria	1.44pm
					Oval	1.50½
					Camberwell Green	1.56
					New Cross Gate	2.08
					Lewisham	2.18½
					Rushey Green	2.24
					Downham	2.30
					Grove Park	2.35½
16 December 1951	'E/3' 169	West Norwood-Manor House	11.00	11.00	West Norwood	4.14pm
					Herne Hill	4.20½
					Lambeth Town Hall	4.26½
					Oval	4.33½
					Savoy St	4.46½
					Angel	4.58
					Balls Pond Road	5.04
					Manor House	5.14
16 March 1952	'E/3' 2003	West Norwood-Charing Cross	5.75	11.13	West Norwood	4.27pm
					Herne Hill	4.33
					Lambeth Town Hall	4.37½
					Oval	4.45
					Charing Cross	4.58
5 April 1952	'E/3' 180	Manor House-West Norwood	11.00	11.38	Manor House	7.41pm
					Balls Pond Road	7.48½
					Angel	7.56½
					Bloomsbury	8.04
					Savoy St	8.09
					Oval	8.23
					Lambeth Town Hall	8.28½
					Herne Hill	8.34
					West Norwood	8.39
5 April 1952	'E/3' 180	West Norwood-Aldwych Tram Station	6.50	11.47	West Norwood	8.45pm
					Herne Hill	8.51½
					Lambeth Town Hall	8.57
					Oval	9.04½
					Aldwych Station	9.19

Distances are in miles, speeds in miles per hour.   The first timing on each run is the departure time, the others the arrival times.

Appendix IV   *London Tramway Accidents, 1946-1951*

A. Analysis of Accidents

Year	Collision (Note 1)	Derailment (Note 2)	Pedestrians Run Down	Other	Total Accidents	Trams Involved	Trams Damaged (Note 3)	Passengers Injured	Staff Injured	Others Injured	Total Injured	Staff Killed	Others Killed	Total Killed
1946	7	4	–	–	11	16	6	29	2	6	37	–	–	–
1947	16	22	–	1	39	48	21	28	7	30	65	–	1	1
1948	16	8	5	1	30	35	12	7	–	10	17	1	2	3
1949	21	5	1	2	29	39	23	52	5	4	61	–	1	1
1950	21	15	3	1	40	48	18	26	5	43	74	1	2	3
1951	18	10	2	2	32	39	13	58	5	56	119	1	1	2
Total	99	64	11	7	181	225	93	200	24	149	373	3	7	10

Note 1: Including collisions followed by derailments.   *Note 2:* Including derailments followed by collisions.   *Note 3:* Conservative estimate only.

B. Accidents per Month

Month	1946	1947	1948	1949	1950	1951	Total
January	–	3	1	4	3	4	15
February	–	3	3	1	4	6	17
March	–	4	2	1	3	3	13
April	4	4	3	1	4	4	20
May	–	2	2	1	4	1	10
June	–	5	2	1	3	2	13
July	3	1	2	3	3	1	13
August	2	1	2	5	10	2	22
September	1	4	3	3	1	5	17
October	–	1	10	–	1	–	12
November	–	6	–	6	3	3	18
December	1	5	–	3	1	1	11
Total	11	39	30	29	40	32	181
Average	1	3	3	2	3	3	15